Celebrating Winter Solstice

Customs and Crafts, Recipes and Rituals
for Festivals of Light, Hanukkah, Yule,
and Other Midwinter Holidays

Compiled by
Waverly Fitzgerald

Genesta Press

Contents

The Crowning Solstice 1
Winter Solstice 3
Birth of the Miraculous Child 6
Night of the Mothers 8
Festival of Lights 17
Magical Gift Givers 20
Goddesses of Solstice 29
Yule Themes and Activities 31
Gift-Giving and Games 37
Celebrating with Food 44
Carols and Poems 59
References 69
About This Book 72

The Crowning Solstice

The Winter Solstice is the shining crown in the galaxy of holidays, especially dazzling in the dark depths of winter, surrounded by the other glittering festal occasions of winter, like St Lucy, her crown of candles glowing, appearing in the pre-dawn darkness, surrounded by the stars.

Yule has been the Old English name of the Midwinter holiday for almost two thousand years; for example, Bede mentions it in the sixth century. I have seen it derived from the word for "wheel" (which seems appropriate at the time of the year, where it shows up in so many ways), or from the same root word as "jovial." But I believe the most widely accepted understanding is that it simply describes the Midwinter feast, often defined as a feast of twelve days. With so many winter holidays and customs related to them, I've chosen to focus on the ones that resonate most closely with the themes of Winter Solstice:

> Birth of the sun:
> Winter Solstice, Sol Invictus
>
> Birth of the miraculous child:
> Christmas, Koreion, Mithra, Modresnacht
>
> Birth of the new year:
> New Year's Day, Saturnalia, Twelve Days
>
> Lighting lights in the darkness:
> Winter Solstice, Hanukkah, Advent, St Lucy
>
> Reversal of usual roles:
> Saturnalia, Hanukkah, Twelfth Night
>
> Magical gift-bringers of the winter skies:
> St Nicholas, Lucia, Frauen, Wild Horde
>
> Goddesses of solstice:
> Our Lady of Guadalupe, Our Lady of Solitude

I recommend supplementing this book with John Matthew's gorgeous book *The Winter Solstice*. Although I've included a few references to this book, it would be a disservice to try to paraphrase his rich interpretations of winter customs. If you are still hungry for more information, several links are provided in the References at the end of this book.

Winter Solstice

The Winter Solstice is unique among days of the year—the shortest day and the longest night. The darkness triumphs, but only briefly. For the solstice is also a turning point. From now on (until the summer solstice, at any rate), the nights grow shorter and the days grow longer, the dark wanes and the Sun waxes in power. From the dark womb of the night, the light is born.

The word solstice means literally "sun stand," describing a phenomenon related to the sun's apparent movement south during the winter. As the sun reaches its southernmost position at the Winter Solstice, it seems to stand still for a few days. Then it turns around and heads north, bringing with it a few more minutes of light every day. The apparent motion of the sun is due to the earth's tilt as it revolves around the sun. At the Winter Solstice, the Northern Hemisphere is tilted away from the sun so the sun seems to be farther south. At summer solstice, by contrast, we are tilted towards the sun, thus enjoying the maximum amount of light. Of course, the opposite conditions exist in the Southern Hemisphere.

The Winter Solstice, like the other solar turning points of the year (the equinoxes and the summer solstice), is determined astrologically, based on the date and time that the sun moves into the constellation of Capricorn, the Mountain Goat. This always falls on one of three days—December 20, 21, or 22. That's why we have to look up the date in a calendar every year.

This turning point was carefully monitored in the most ancient cultures. The stones in the circle at Stonehenge were aligned to ascertain the dates of midsummer and midwinter, as well as the positions of the moon throughout the year. Even older than Stonehenge is the tumulus at Newgrange in the Boyne River Valley in Ireland. It was built in approximately 4,500 BCE, making it six thousand years old. On the morning of Winter Solstice, a shaft of sunlight enters the mound, traveling down a stone corridor and illuminating the spiral designs on the back wall of the cave. Patricia Monaghan describes what it is like to be present at this moment:

> At 8:55, a dim strip of light appears on the sandy floor of the cave. The watchers gasp, for the light seems to arrive in a rush, not to creep into the cavern. For a few moments the inch-wide strip rests there. Eyes begin to adjust to the new brightness. Then, the light begins to change color and to widen. Within moments a wide strip of butter-yellow light blasts across the cave, reflecting upwards sufficiently to illuminate the rough corbeled arch twenty feet above. The light glows like fire.
>
> The sunlight pours in, warming the cave's occupants with its color. One by one they kneel in the sand and put their hands into the light. Everyone is surprised, for far from being as warm as its tawny color suggests, the light is cool. Everyone peers down the corridor into the light. Almost everyone weeps. There is little talk; the feeling of a sacred presence is so strong that words evaporate.

The light withdraws from the cave slowly. A half hour later the waiters emerge from the cave to see the sun just risen above the horizon.

> Witnesses report an odd sensation of knowing, for the first time, that there is light behind them as well as in front of their eyes. There is a feeling that light and air are separate—the sense that light is rarer, more precious. And there is the added sense that the sunlight is a living, conscious entity, a feeling that begins in the darkness of the cave but does not end for hours, sometimes days, afterwards.

There is lively debate about the purpose of this ancient stone construction, apparently created to celebrate this particular moment in time. Some scholars believe it is a ritual site for enacting the fertilization of the earth by the male sun-god. Monaghan, who has written a whole book to bring to light the long-forgotten myths of a female sun-goddess, suggests that the large stone basins found in the cavern were filled with water and became mirrors in which the sun could admire her beauty, just as seeing her radiance in a magic mirror brought the Japanese sun goddess Amateratsu out of her cave.

John Matthews, in his book *The Winter Solstice,* mentions other ancient sites where the solstice sunrise is marked. In Chaco Canyon in New Mexico, the solstice sunrise creates the shape of two daggers flanking a spiral on a cliff face. At the Mayan site of Kukulkan in Chichen Itza, the first rays of Winter Solstice crawl down the steps of the pyramid, forming the shape of a serpent that eventually connects to the head of a serpent carved at the foot of the steps.

Birth of the Sun

Winter Solstice was celebrated as the birth of the sun, the birth of light, the birth of life. The ancient Persians set bonfires on this day and their rulers sent birds aloft bearing torches of dried grass to stimulate the sun.

Sol Invictus

The Romans celebrated two different sun holidays in December. The *Agonia* on December 11 honored the ancient Sun god, Sol Indiges (*indiges* being from the same root word as indigenous). On December 25, the Romans recognized the birth of Sol Invictus, the Unconquered Sun, definitely the sun returning triumphantly from the darkness of midwinter.

Itiwanna

The Zuni and Hopi people of southwestern North America also honor the Winter Solstice with ceremonies. Zuni houses contain plates on the walls that are lit by the rays of the sun passing through a small window only one day a year: on Winter Solstice. After the Pekwin or Sun Priest of the Zuni announces the exact moment of the *itiwanna,* the rebirth of the sun, twelve kachina clowns appear to perform a ritual dance along with effigies of twelve-foot tall birds that were seen as messengers of the gods. The Hopi also celebrate the rebirth of the sun with an all-night ceremony called the Prayer-offering ceremony. The Solstice day was a "day of good will, when every man wishes for prosperity and health, for his family and friends," wrote the anthropologist Edmund Nequatewa in 1931.

Birth of the Miraculous Child

Of course, the date the sun was reborn worked wonderfully well as a metaphor for the birth of other miraculous heroes and children who brought new life into the world.

Mithra

As the cult of the Persian hero and god Mithra grew, he became assimilated with the sun, and his birth was celebrated on the sun's birthday: December 25. The myth tells us that he sprang up full-grown from a rock, armed with a knife and carrying a torch.

Shepherds watched Mithra's miraculous appearance and hurried to greet him with the first fruits of their flocks and their harvests. Sound familiar? His cult spread throughout Roman lands during the second century.

Aeon

Another miraculous child born to a virgin at this time of year was the child Aeon, born to the goddess Kore on January 6. This seems to have been celebrated with a festival called the Koreion in Alexandria.

St Epiphanius complains about the hideous mockery of this rite, but it was probably much older than the story of Christ's birth. The image of the goddess, decorated with gold stars, was carried seven times around her temple as the priests cried, "The Virgin has brought forth the Aeon!" Although Aeon, or Eon, is now defined as "an indefinitely long period of time; an age; an eternity," its Indo-European root *aiw* conveyed "vital force, life, long life, eternity" and the Greek form *Aion* meant specifically "vital force." Aeon was another Year God.

The description of the Koreion contains the same elements as the Egyptian ceremony enacting the birth of Horus, the Sun-God, to Isis. All lights in the city were doused while Isis circled the sarcophagus seven times, then brought forth Horus, who was called "The Light of the World." Statues of Isis holding the newly born sun god on her lap, presenting him to the world, are similar in pose to later statues depicting the Madonna and Child.

Horus

According to Normandi Ellis, the ancient Egyptians also used the Winter Solstice as the date for the birth of the Sun (known as Ra in lower Egypt and Horus in upper Egypt). Ellis notes that there once was an immense sycamore tree at the desert's edge in Heliopolis, where it was said that Isis stopped to suckle Horus when she was hiding from Seth, who was trying to kill her and her baby. The same tree shrine was visited by Christian pilgrims, who said it was the place Mary rested and suckled the Christ child on their flight from Egypt.

Christ Child

The metaphor of the birth of the sun worked equally well for Christians celebrating the birth of the Son of God, who brings Light to the world. Biblical scholars speculate that Christ was actually born in the fall after the harvest or in the spring after the birth of the new animals, both the most likely times for taxation. The British scientist Colin Humphreys believes Christ was born between April 13 and April 27, during the week of Passover in 5 BC, when a great comet appeared.

The early church celebrated the birth of Christ on January 6. However, in the fourth century, the celebration was moved to December 25. Biblical scholar Brent Walters says that the pope authorized this change at the request of Cyril of Jerusalem, who was concerned about the pilgrims who flocked to Jerusalem to celebrate Christ's birth, then turned around and headed to Bethlehem to attend the special ceremonies there on the same day. By moving the date of Christ's birth forward to December 24, they had more time to make the trip to Bethlehem by January 6. Of course, not everyone was happy with this change. The Christians of Edessa accused the church in Rome of idolatry and "sun worship."

Night of the Mothers

The Venerable Bede, writing about the customs of the pagan Anglo-Saxons he was trying to convert in sixth century England, mentions their practice of celebrating a holiday he called *Modranicht* (or *Modresnacht*) on the eve of Christmas. This "night of the Mothers" was evidently a sacred night devoted to a group of feminine divinities, perhaps those pictured on carvings and statues all over Celtic France and Britain, which show three women together, holding children and fruit, fish, grain, and other bounties of the earth.

Marina Warner in her book about the cult of the Virgin Mary includes an image which depicts a similar scene in Rome, painted in a niche in the church of St Maria Antiqua. It shows St Anne holding the child Mary and St Elizabeth holding the infant John the Baptist, on either side of the Madonna and Child, "a triple goddess with her miraculous offspring."

Hanukkah

The Jewish festival of light, Hanukkah, begins on the 25th day of Kislev, three days before the new moon closest to the Winter Solstice. This means it spans the darkest time of the year both in the lunar cycle and the solar cycle.

Hanukkah commemorates the victory of the Maccabees against the Hellenistic overseers of Israel, who outlawed Jewish religious practices while reinstating pagan rituals. In 166 BCE, the Maccabees recaptured Jerusalem. They chose the 26th of Kislev as the day to purify and rededicate the temple, which had been desecrated three years earlier. The explanation for the emphasis on lighting candles is explained by recounting the miracle of the oil, how one jar of oil kept the lamps lit for the eight days of the festival. But, as Arthur Waskow points out, the Greeks were probably celebrating a Winter Solstice ritual on that day. By claiming the same day for their festival, the Maccabees were rededicating not only the temple but also the day itself to Jewish holiness. They were capturing a pagan solstice festival that had won wide support among partially Hellenized Jews, in order to make it a day of God's victory over paganism. Even the lighting of candles for Hanukkah fits the context of the surrounding torchlight honors for the sun.

The main practice of Hanukkah is the lighting of the candles in the menorah, one each night, until on the eighth night all eight candles are lit. Both men and women are forbidden to work during the time it takes the candles to burn each night. In some Sephardic communities, women do not work at all on the first and eighth days of Hanukkah, and in some places, they don't work on any of the eight days. Just as the Sabbath is the day for rest provided during the week, so are the eight days of Hanukkah a mandatory resting time at this pivotal point in the year.

Saturnalia

The Roman festival of Saturnalia was celebrated for seven days, from December 17 to December 24. It honored the corn-god Saturn and his consort, Ops, the goddess of plenty. Normal activities were suspended during this time period. No wars were fought. No business was conducted. Schools and courts were closed. People spent their time gambling and feasting. Roles were reversed, with masters waiting on their servants. Everyone was free to say exactly what they pleased without fear of the consequences, so this was a time for great ventilation of feelings and political satire. For an ancient account of this day, and the Roman calendar in general, Blackburn and Holford-Strevens recommend reading Macrobius, who describes an imaginary debate among pagan intellectuals taking place on Saturnalia, possibly in 383 AD.

Teresa Ruano, at her wonderful website Candlegrove, reproduces this passage from *The Epistolae of Seneca the Younger*, who was writing about Saturnalia around 50 AD:

> It is now the month of December, when the greatest
> part of the city is in a bustle. Loose reins are given to
> public dissipation; everywhere you may hear the
> sound of great preparations, as if there were some real

difference between the days devoted to Saturn and those for transacting business... Were you here, I would willingly confer with you as to the plan of our conduct; whether we should live in our usual way, or, to avoid singularity, both take a better supper and throw off the toga.

The Greek god equivalent to Saturn is Cronus. Saturn carries a sickle, like the Grim Reaper. Cronos, who ate his own children rather than let them surpass him, gives his name to terms like chronological. Both are time-gods, who bring death and limitation and may fight to preserve their reign, even though they know it is time for them to be replaced with new life, just as the old year must die to give way to the new, a struggle depicted in many Winter Solstice customs, such as mummers plays and the *pastorelas*, satiric plays performed in Mexico that depict a battle between angels and devils.

A Lord of Misrule was often elected to mock the role of authority and direct his followers in ribald and humorous activities. Some folklorists (Frazer and Graves) believe he was a stand-in for the king and was sacrificed at the end of the time period in the king's place. During his brief reign of thirty days, the Lord of Misrule assumed the king's prerogatives, dressing in royal robes, doing anything he wanted, and commanding obedience.

People gave gifts to each other, usually small items such as candles, terra cotta dolls, or sprigs of holly, symbolizing wishes for the new year.

The day following the Saturnalia was the Juvenilia which, according to Z Budapest in *The Grandmother of Time,* was a holiday in honor of children, who were entertained, feasted, and given talismans such as bells, shoes, warm clothes, and toys for good luck in the coming year. This makes sense. After vanquishing the Old King, it's time to celebrate the new in the form of children, the New Year's Baby, the Son of Man.

Twelfth Night

> Now Christmas is past,
> Twelfth Night is the last
> To the Old Year adieu,
> Great joy to the new.

This twelfth night of the twelve days of Christmas is the official end of the winter holiday season and one of the traditional days for taking down the Christmas decorations. This is also a traditional day for wassailing apple trees. In southern and western England, revelers gathered in orchards, where they sang to the trees, drank to their health, poured hot cider over their roots, left cider-soaked toast in their branches for the birds, and scared away evil spirits with a great shout and the firing of guns.

The ancient Roman tradition of choosing the master of the Saturnalia revels by baking a good-luck bean inside a cake was transferred to Twelfth Night. In Italy, the beans were hidden in *focaccia* rather than a cake: three white beans for the Magi and one black one. Whoever found the black bean was made king and could choose his queen and rule the banquet. In colonial Virginia, a great ball was held on this night. The king wins the honor of sponsoring the ball the following year; the queen, the privilege of making next year's Twelfth Night Cake.

This final day of the Christmas season was considered the beginning of Carnival in Italy, where it was associated with jokes and tricks. In Tuscany, a man used to dress up like a witch called Befana and surround himself with *befanotti*, low-life characters wearing false beards and inside-out jackets. Booths were set up in the piazzas, offering toys and games. Vendors dressed up young boys like women, with blackened faces, caps on their heads, a long reed in one hand, a lantern in the other, and hung them with baskets of oranges and golden pine cones. All of these resemble Saturnalia customs, and Twelfth Night does partake of the quality of Saturnalia with its emphasis on light-hearted fun, social satire, and role reversals.

Epiphany

The Epiphany (which means apparition or manifestation) honors the arrival of the Magi and the first public presentation of the Baby Jesus. In Belgium, children dress up as the Three Kings and go from door to door singing a begging song. In Spain, the Magi leave gifts in the shoes that children have filled with straw and grain for the camels and set out on balconies or by the front door the previous evening. Children who awaken to find a charcoal mark on their face are said to have been kissed by Balthazar.

Since the twelve nights of Christmas are a liminal time when evil spirits, like the Greek *kalikatzari*, can roam the earth, people protect their houses by chalking the Three Kings' initials on their doors: C or K (in Hungary G), B, and M (for Caspar, Balthazar, and Melchoir).

In Bulgaria, housewives rise early and carry the family crucifix, icons, and plough to the village fountain. There they wash them with salt and water, saying, "May the wheat be as white as the plough, as wholesome as the salt." The clergy also bless homes with holy water. If the water freezes on the priest's boxwood whisk, the year will be good and the crops fruitful.

In Danube port towns, they bless the waters. In Philippopolis, the most important town of southern Bulgaria, the priest throws the cross from the bridge into the Maritza River. The man who recovers it is allowed to take it around from house to house and receive money gifts, then returns it to the priest, who bestows his blessing.

Italians believe that animals can talk on the night of Epiphany, so owners feed them well. Fountains and rivers in Calabria run with olive oil and wine, and everything turns briefly into something to eat: the walls into ricotta, the bedposts into sausages, and the sheets into lasagna. This is also the wonder night of the year in Syria where it is said that trees bow at midnight in honor of the Christ child, and miracles of increase occur.

This was the original date when the birth of Christ was celebrated, and even now the Armenians celebrate both the Nativity and the Baptism of Christ on this day by eating fried fish, lettuce, and boiled spinach, supposedly the foods the Virgin Mary ate on the night before she gave birth.

During the week before Epiphany, Italian children sometimes dress up and go in groups of three, carrying a pole with a golden star on top, and stopping at houses to sing *pasquelle*, little songs about the coming of the Magi. Sometimes they are given money, but other places they receive gifts of food: sausages, bread, eggs, dried figs, and wine. In some small rustic towns, the Nativity is re-enacted on Epiphany Eve with the newest baby in town taking the part of Jesus.

In Friuli, families gather around the hearth to watch the Christmas log burn. For centuries, bonfires have been lit to light the way for the Three Kings. The fires are called *pan e vin*, bread and wine, or *vecja*, old one. Boys run through the fields carrying burning brands, jump across the fires, and roll burning wheels down the hill, shouting out the names of their fiancées as a way to announce their engagements.

Carol Field describes an Epiphany procession in the town of Tarcento that ascends a hill to where a huge bonfire is set up, made of sheaves of corn, brambles of brushwood, and pine branches. The fire is lit by the oldest man and ignites firecrackers and fireworks while bells ring in the town. The way the smoke blows foretells the prospects for the coming year: smoke blowing east predicts a year of abundance while smoke blowing west is a bad omen for the crops. People take home embers to fertilize their fields; the embers are magically said to transform into sacks of wheat.

In some places, a straw effigy of the Befana is placed on the fire and burned as a way of getting rid of the old year. Sometimes chestnuts are thrown on the fire and roasted, as a symbol of fertility.

Traditional foods served in Friuli on Epiphany Eve include mulled wine and *pinza*, a rustic sweet bread, made with corn flour (or sometimes rye and wheat), filled with raisins and pine nuts and figs, spiced with fennel seeds, and shaped like a simple round or a Greek epsilon with three arms of equal length. It was once cooked under the embers. It is considered good luck to eat *pinza* made by seven different families.

In Ireland, Epiphany is called Women's Christmas, a day for women to get together with their friends and sisters and relax after the grueling work of the holidays.

Advent

The period of Advent, which means "to come," is the period of waiting for the birth of Christ at Christmas, or for the birth of the sun at Winter Solstice. It is a period of anticipation, of looking forward.

The main quality of Advent is waiting. Most Advent customs have to do with marking time: lighting one candle on the Advent wreath each week, opening another door on the Advent calendar, setting out the figures in the creche, adding ornaments to a Jesse tree. These markers show us in a concrete way how much time has passed and how much time is left before the event we so joyously anticipate.

In Mexico during the nine nights before Christmas, children re-enact the drama of Mary and Joseph searching for room at the inn. This custom is called *Las Posadas* (which means inn or shelter). One child dressed as an angel heads the procession, followed by two people dressed as Mary and Joseph (or carrying statues of Mary and Joseph) followed by others carrying lighted candles. At each home, they sing a *vilancicos*, a medieval Spanish carol, which features improvised lines by the members of the group. *"En nombre del ciel,"* they beg ("in heaven's name"), but the reply is always *"Marchad a otra parte, y buena venture"* ("move on elsewhere and good luck"), until they read a house where one family sings *"Pase la escogida"* ("Let the chosen one enter").

Once inside, they place their lighted candles around the *nascimiento* (nativity scene) and say a prayer and a blessing for their generous hosts. Then it's time for a party featuring fruit, hot punch, *bunelos* (pastries), and sometimes tamales or pozole (a thick, stew-like dish).

In some parts of Mexico, a pinata is broken on each of the nine nights of Las Posadas. In other places, it is broken only on Christmas Eve. The pinata, made of paper mâché applied over a clay pot, is filled with treats including nuts, fresh limes, sugar canes, and small green fruits.

Pastorelas, shepherds' plays, are also performed during this time. These plays were introduced by Franciscan friars. A group of shepherds start towards Bethlehem but are tempted by devils. Angels rush in to rescue the shepherds and drive off the devils. These plays feature singing, dancing, and satire, much like the medieval English mummers' plays, which were often performed during the winter holidays.

Twelve Days

In Babylon, the twelve intercalary days between the Winter Solstice and the New Year were seen as the time of a struggle between chaos and order, with chaos trying to take over the world.

Other cultures (Hindu, Chinese, Celtic) also viewed this as a time for reversing order and rules.

This idea survives in the celebration of the Twelve Days of Christmas, which end on January 6 with Twelfth Night. In Wales, they were considered "omen" days. In Scotland, no court had power during the twelve days. The Irish believed that anyone who died during these days escaped purgatory and went straight to Heaven.

In medieval England, all work was suspended during the Christmas holidays. Women could begin spinning again on January 7, the day after Twelfth Night, which was called St Distaff's Day. According to Germanic tradition, the goddess Holle, dressed all in white, rides the wind in a wagon on the Twelve Days of Christmas. During this time, no wheels can turn: no spinning, no milling, no wagons (sleighs were used instead). Holle punishes women who disobeyed the taboo. Women were also forbidden to work on the days of certain female saints whose holidays fall during the winter. Lacemakers and spinners take a holiday on November 25, St Catherine's Day. And any woman who works on St Lucy's Day (December 13) will find her work undone the next day.

Helen Farias suggests that the twelve days were originally thirteen nights, celebrated from the dark moon nearest the solstice through the next full moon. Greek women celebrated a Dionysian ritual on the full moon nearest the Winter Solstice.

The Greeks told a story about the halcyon days, the two-week period before and after the solstice, when the kingfisher built her nest on the waves and the sea was calm while she hatched her chicks. Aristotle refers to a poem about this time written by Simonides of Ceos: "when in the winter month Zeus brings calm to fourteen days that earthlings call the time when the wind is forgotten, the holy breeding-season of the many-colored alcyon."

Shakespeare refers to this legend in this passage from *Hamlet* (I, i 157):

Some say that ever 'gainst that season comes
Wherein our Saviour's birth is celebrated,
The bird of dawning singeth all night long;
And then, they say, no spirit can walk abroad;

The nights are wholesome; then no planets strike,
No fairy takes, nor witch hath power to charm,
So hallow'd and so gracious is the time.

Festival of Lights

The return of the light is the most prominent feature of most midwinter festivals. By lighting lights in the darkness, we celebrate the birth of the sun, stimulate the growing strength of the light, and illuminate the darkness.

Christmas Candle

The Christmas candle was once a popular part of the Christmas tradition in Great Britain, Ireland, and Scandinavia. A large candle, usually red or some other bright color, was decorated with holly or other evergreens. One person, usually the eldest or the head of the household, is designated as the light-bringer. She lit the candle for the first time on Christmas Eve before the festive supper and during each of the remaining evenings of the Twelve Days of Christmas. To extinguish the candle after the meal or at bedtime, she snuffed it with tongs rather than blowing it out, since that would blow the luck away. The candle shed a blessing on the household, and so its light was protected from accidental quenching.

It seems likely that the candle also represented the coming year, just as the weather of each of the twelve days of Christmas foretells the weather of the corresponding month. It had protective or fertilizing powers and was kept as a charm. In Denmark, during a lightning storm, the remnant would be brought out and lit to protect the household.

Yule Log

Similar customs once surrounded the Yule log. The Yule log must never be bought, but rather should be received as a gift or found or taken from your own property. Often the log to be burned at midwinter is chosen early in the year and set aside.

Tradition varies about the type of wood to be used. Oak logs were popular in the north of England, birch in Scotland, and ash in Cornwall and Devon. Ash is the only wood that burns freely when green and the world-tree, Yggdrasil, in the Nordic tradition was an ash-tree. It is important that the Yule log be the biggest and greenest log available, since the Christmas festivities will last only as long as the Yule log burns.

In some parts of the Scottish Highlands, the head of the household finds a withered stump and carves it into the likeness of an old woman, the *Cailleach Nollaich* or Christmas Old Wife, a sinister being representing the evils of winter and death. She's the goddess of winter, the hag of night, the old one who brings death. Burning her drives away the winter and protects the occupants of the household from death.

The Yule log is first brought into the house with great ceremony on Christmas Eve (or the eve of solstice, if one prefers), decorated with holly and ivy and other evergreens. Some people prefer to use the Yule log as a decoration and place candles on it instead, thus transforming it into a candelabra, like the menorah or the kinara. It is lit with a piece of last year's log as described in Herrick's poem, "Hesperides":

> Come bring with a noise
> My merry, merry boys
> The Christmas log to the firing
> With the last year's brand.
> Light the new block,
> And for good success in his spending
> On your psalteries play:
> That sweet luck may
> Come while the log is a-teendling.

In Italy, the Yule log is called the *Ceppo*. Boccaccio in the fourteenth century described a Florentine family gathering about the hearth and pouring a libation of wine upon the glowing wood, then sharing the remaining wine, thus linking the Yule log with the custom of wassailing, pouring out libations to the trees in the orchard.

The Yule log is left to burn all night, and, if possible, through the next twelve without going out, although it may be extinguished with water. It is treated with great respect. No one touches it with dirty hands and, in medieval England, people who passed touched their hats to it. The ashes are kept for good luck. They have magical properties and can be scattered in the field to fertilize the soil or sprinkled around the house for protection.

Lighting the Menorah

The traditional menorah has eight lights in a row, with none higher than the other. Since the lights are not to be used for any practical purpose, it became customary to add a ninth candle, a *shammas* or *shammash*, which is often set above the others and used to light them. The candles are lit as soon as possible after the stars come out each evening and are left to burn for a half an hour.

On the first night, one candle is put into the menorah, on the far right, and the *shammas* is lit. Three blessings are said before the *shammas* is used to light the candle. The blessings acknowledge the Lord God, who commands us to light candles for Hanukkah, who worked miracles for our ancestors in this season, who has given us life, lifted us up and brought us to this season. Unlike other Jewish traditions, women are also obligated to light Hanukkah candles. In some households, there is a separate menorah for each family member. The menorah should be placed in an outside window so it can be seen from outside, although if this is dangerous, it can be placed on a table in the room.

After the candles are lit, several songs are sung, including this one:

> We kindle these lights on account of the miracles, the wonders, the liberations, and the battles that You carried out for our forebears in these days at this time of year, through the hands of Your holy priests. For all eight days of Hanukkah these lights are holy. We are not allowed to use them; they are only to look at, in order to thank and praise your great Name on account of Your miracles, Your wonders, and Your liberations. [Waskow, p. 95]

Magical Gift Givers

Although most Americans are only familiar with Santa Claus, in Europe there are a number of masculine and feminine spirits who bring gifts to children during the holiday season.

In France, gifts come from Pere Noel, and sometimes the Child Jesus, le petit Noel. Russian children look forward to visits from Grandfather Frost. Scandinavian kids pour out sour cream for the *Jule-Nisse*, a small gnome that lives on a farm and gives gifts like Santa Claus. On Christmas Day in Bulgaria, Grandfather Koleda presents gifts to the children. In Finland, gifts are presented by Wainamoinen, the hero of the Kalevala, or by Ukko, a mythological character who is depicted as being an elderly gentleman with a long white mustache, wearing a white cap with blue bands and a red coat. In Greece, St Basil is the gift-bestowing patron saint on New Year's Day. Likewise, the Armenian gift-giver, Gaghant Bab, comes on New Year's Day.

In other countries, the Wise Men bring gifts on Epiphany. In Syria, the youngest camel that accompanied the Wise Men is called the Camel of Jesus and presents the gifts. In Spain, the children stuff their shoes with straw and put them outside. The following morning, the Magi's' horses have eaten the straw and left behind toys, cookies, and other gifts. In Italy, Befana fills children's stockings on the evening before January 6, her special day. In Sicily, gifts come from *la Vecchia di Natali*, the old Woman of Christmas. Exactly the same old lady, but called Babushka, makes the Epiphany rounds in Russia.

In Switzerland, a holiday couple walk about distributing gifts: St Lucy and Father Christmas. In Sweden, sometimes two masked people distribute gifts, an old woman and an old man. She produces sealed packages from her basket while the old man rings the bell he carries.

In Hungary, children are brought their gifts by the angels, while in Poland it is the stars that descend to do this important job. The Mother Star is impersonated by a woman in a white robe and veil, attended by a Father Star who first tests the children on their hymns and prayers before handing out gifts.

In Franche-Comte, *Tante Aria* arrives riding on an ass and bestows gifts. *Tante Aria* is the Air of Wine Mother. Hottes believes she is the cloud goddess, mentioned in the Rig Veda, who is brought in a cart drawn by asses to wed the moon-god at the Winter Solstice.

St Nicholas / Santa Claus

Santa Claus is the most familiar of the Yule gift givers in America. Behind the jolly figure of the old man with the white beard and the red-and-white suit is a fourth century bishop, St Nicholas. And behind him lurk the memories of older deities.

In the Netherlands, on the eve of St Nicholas (December 5), children put out carrots and hay for St Nicholas's horse and wooden shoes (or sometimes baskets) by the mantle. St Nicholas rides through the air on his white horse and comes down the chimney to fill them with treats.

Czech kids believe St Nicholas comes down a golden cord carrying a basket of apples, nuts, and candies. In Hungary, the shoes are left outside the window. In France, children hang stockings near the fire and say this prayer:

> Saint Nicholas, mon bon patron,
> Envoyez-moi quelque chose de bon.

Sometimes St Nicholas is summoned to appear in person. In the Netherlands, children sing special songs welcoming him and spread a white sheet on the ground. The door suddenly opens and a shower of goodies falls on the sheet. Then St Nicholas appears, dressed in his ecclesiastical robes, and questions the children about their behavior. He is accompanied by *Zwarte Piet*, or Black Peter the Moor, who carries a thick rod and a sack and threatens to carry the children off if they are bad.

In Austria, as well, St Nicholas makes rounds dressed in glittering bishop's robes. He has a long white beard and carries a pastoral staff. While he rewards good children with nuts and sweets, naughty youngsters are taunted with a switch by his black-faced servant. In some parts of Austria, this character is called *Laubauf*, a horned monster. In the Austrian state of Styria, he is called *Bartlell*. In lower Austria, *Krampus* or *Grampus*. In Czechoslovakia, St Nicholas is accompanied by an angel and a devil. The mumming plays performed in medieval England at winter time often featured a figure called Father Christmas, who gave gifts and threw trinkets, as well as a Moor.

We know very little about the saint who loaned his name to Santa Claus, which is a corruption of the Dutch *Sinte* (Saint) *Klaus*. Nicholas lived around the year 325 and was a bishop of Myra in Asia Minor (near the current Finke in Turkey). In 1087, Italian sailors and merchants brought his relics (some say they stole them, which is one reason St Nicholas is the patron saint of thieves) from his tomb in Asia Minor to Bari in Italy, where a great shrine grew up around them. In time, Nelson comments "a host of legends, icons, songs, plays, and folk practices" grew up around him, as elaborate as his shrine. Most of these stories revolve around his spectacular gift-giving.

In one story, St Nicholas takes pity on three daughters of a poor man who have decided to turn to prostitution since they have no hope of marrying without dowries. He throws three golden balls through the window, thus enabling them to marry happily. The three balls became his emblem.

It may be possible that depictions of this miracle gave rise to another story about how St Nicholas restored to life three boys who had been cut up by a greedy innkeeper and put into a vat (the balls being mistaken for heads, as Juno Lucina's cakes were mistaken for St Lucy's eyes). Matthews believes this reflects an older understanding of St Nicholas as a shaman who experiences ritual dismemberment and resurrection.

Another legend tells how he begged some grain from a ship passing through Myra during a famine. He kept some and baked the rest as bread, in his shape. Thus, he is the patron of bakers. And perhaps the creator of gingerbread men.

The Syrians say that when shipwrecked, St Nicholas sailed safely over the stormy seas in his hat. Another legend tells how he rescued three sailors from a violent storm off the coast of Turkey, thus becoming the patron of sailors. In fact, his feast day is more popular with sailors than with children in Italy and Greece. Greek sailors light a candle before the icon of St Nicholas found on every ship and say prayers for safe passage. In Bari, Italy, on his feast day, the image of St Nicholas is placed in a boat decorated with flowers and banners, which is taken far out to sea, then returned to its shrine at night.

His association with the sea suggests that some of his stories may have evolved from stories told about Poseidon, whose month this is, in the Athenian and Roman calendars. Farther north, it seems his figure merged with that of Woden. Old Nick is another name for Woden, who like the Celtic Holly King, is the lord of the dead. St Nick is often pictured riding a white horse like Odin's Sleipnir. He lives in the North, the dwelling place of spirits and the dead.

Santa Lucia

In Italy, Santa Lucia (Loo-CEE-a) is the gift-giver who comes in the night, like St Nicholas or Santa Claus. Children leave bunches of carrots, hay, and bowls of milk for the donkey on which she travels around the countryside. In Bergamo and the surrounding country-side, children leave their shoes on the kitchen window with hay, and in the morning, they find tiny sweets the size of a coin tied to their shoelaces.

St Lucy is a Sicilian saint, the patroness of Syracuse, where she was martyred in the reign of Diocletian. One story says that when a suitor admired her beautiful eyes, she cut them out and sent them to him, asking to be left in peace thereafter (like most early Christian virgin martyrs, she refused marriage). Now she is the patron of eye diseases and the blind, and she is often depicted carrying her eyeballs on a plate.

Lucy means "light." Lucina is the Sabine goddess of Light, often pictured holding a plate of cakes (later mistaken for eyeballs) and a lamp. She was later absorbed into an aspect of Juno, Juno Lucina, who is goddess of childbirth. Lucina is usually shown carrying a tray and a lamp; her title is "opener of the eyes," referring to her role as midwife. Since Lucy's day falls right before (or, before the calendar change, upon) the Winter Solstice, she can be seen as the midwife of the miraculous sun-child who is born at Yule.

In Italy, her feast day is celebrated with torchlight processions and bonfires, clear indications of her role as light bringer. Apparently untroubled by the gruesome imagery, Italians eat St Lucy's eyes: cakes or biscotti shaped like eyeballs.

In honor of a miracle performed by St Lucy during a famine in 1582 (she made a flotilla of grain-bearing ships appear in the harbor; the people were so hungry they boiled and ate the grain without grinding it into flour), Sicilians don't eat anything made with wheat flour on her day, which means giving up both pasta and bread.

The celebration of St Lucy spread over Europe. But the place where she is most beloved is Scandinavia, where light is especially welcome in the long hours of winter darkness. There, her customs mingle with the traditional deities of the land and ceremonies celebrating the light in the darkness.

In Sweden, in the province of Hallan, according to old records, young women went from farm to farm all through the night, carrying torches to light their way and offering baked goods at each farm they visited, returning home at dawn. In the Scandinavian countries, threshing was supposed to be finished by Lucia's Day, so sometimes people worked all night and were rewarded for their efforts with food and drink.

Granquist notes the similarity between the Italian story of St Lucy sending a ship of wheat to Syracuse and the Scandinavian story in which a magical ship arrives in the middle of a famine, sailing across Lake Vannern, with a glowing woman dressed all in white at the helm. It is St Lucy, bringing food to the starving people. This is one of the tales Helen Farias retells most beautifully, restoring the identity of the magical woman to Freya in her tale for the Advent Sunwheel, "The Ice Ship."

In Sweden, the eldest (or youngest) daughter rises before dawn on St Lucy's Day and fixes a breakfast of special pastries and coffee for her family. She appears in their bedrooms, dressed in a white dress belted with a red sash and wearing a wreath of greens with four lighted candles.

Sometimes the wreath is made of green rue and decorated with red ribbons. She serves traditional pastries called *lussekatter* (or

Lucy cats), x-shaped pastries, sometimes flavored with saffron. These yellow-colored rolls have four arms that curl inward, forming a swastika, a symbol of the sun. Other traditional foods served in her honor include saffron buns, ginger biscuits, and glogg, a hot spiced wine with aquavit.

Later in the day, St Lucy makes a public appearance. Christina Hole describes a typical Swedish procession: St Lucy wearing her crown (of lingonberries or whortleberry twigs and surmounted with seven or nine candles) processes around the village followed by her attendants (young girls clad in white with glitter in their hair), star-boys (wearing white shirts and tall cone-shaped hats decorated with stars), and other children dressed as trolls and demons and old men. Sometimes St Stephen (represented by a man on horseback) leads the way.

In Switzerland, St Lucy strolls around the village with Father Christmas, giving gifts to the girls while he gives gifts to the boys.

Just as the Italian Santa Lucia partakes of the qualities of Juno Lucina, the midwife aspect of Juno the Queen of Heaven, the Scandinavian St Lucia (pronounced LOO-sha) partakes of the qualities of Freya, Queen of Heaven, the Shining Bride.

Helen Farias speculates that the constellation we now know as Orion was once viewed by Celts as the great goddess Bride (the girl representing Lucy is called the *Lussibruden*, the Lucy Bride), and by the Northerners as the goddess Freya. (Orion's belt was sometimes called "Freya's Distaff"). Many centuries ago, this constellation crossed the sky during the winter nights, setting in the west at dawn, about the time the daughter dresses herself as Lucy. (Now, Orion reappears in the North American sky in December.) Freya traveled across the sky in a chariot drawn by cats. Perhaps Lucy's celebration replaced earlier rites devoted to Freya, thus explaining the Lucy cats and the star-boys.

The names for Lucy in Old Norse and in Latin are based on the same root word for light. Hence, Lucia was sometimes linked with Lucifer. In Norway, Lucy is considered a loose woman, even a goblin, and is said to lead the Wild Hunt. Another tale says she was the first wife of Adam, and the mother of the *vittra* people who live underground. Some say the *lussikatter* (Lucy cats) served on her day represent the devil's cats. which the saint subdued so that they gathered around her feet.

The Frauen

The most interesting of all the midwinter goddesses are the Germanic goddesses known as the *Frauen* (or Ladies). The most prominent of these is Frau Perchta (whose name is also spelled Perhte or Berta). Perchta is described as a rather fearsome looking hag, with a long white beard. She rides a goat whose name is Ashurskeggi. She punishes sloppy spinners by ripping out their stomachs, and she blinds those who spy on her. The twelfth day of Christmas is her day, and pancakes and milk are eaten in her honor on January 6. [from Helen Farias]

In parts of the Alps, the *Perhtenlaufen* prevail during the Twelve Days of Christmas. Men dressed in bells and masks run about at night raising an uproar through the streets, led by—or feeling from—the Perhte herself, wildest of all. As in virtually all mumming bands in Europe, this female character is played by a male. According to Miles, in Bavaria three women called *Berchten* would "clear way the evils" by going about the village in the evening of January 5, wearing linen bags with eye, nose, and mouth holes. One carried a rake, one a chain, and one a broom. They would go from house to house and knock with the chain, scrape (the doorstep) with the rake, and sweep with the broom. A purification, clearly. In Carinthia, the *Berchtel* goes dressed in a hide and a hideous wooden mask, hopping about wildly, asking how the children have behaved and demanding gifts rather than bestowing them.

This same goddess appears in another aspect (and under a variation of her name) in a German folk custom recorded by Hottes, who says that yeast cakes baked in the form of a slipper were called the slippers of Hertha. These were filled with small gifts, apparently the forerunner of the custom of leaving out shoes for St Nicholas to fill or stockings for Santa Claus.

> During the Winter Solstice houses were decked with fir and evergreens to welcome her coming. When the family and serfs were gathered to dine, a great altar of flat stones was erected and a fire of fir boughs was

laid. Hertha descended through the smoke, guiding those who were wise in saga lore to foretell the fortunes of those persons at the feast. Hertha's altar stones became the hearthstones of the home.

We learn from this story the reason why Santa Claus comes down the chimney instead of in at the door. It is only a survival of the coming of Hertha in pre-Christian days.

Frau Holle, the twin sister of Perchta, is described as a white lady who rides on the wind in a wagon during the twelve days of Christmas. A braided loaf of bread called *Hollenzopf*, Holla's Braid, was sacrificed to her at Christmas time, according to Gimbutas in *The Language of the Goddess*. She is probably derived from the Norse goddess Hel, the Queen of the Underworld.

The Wild Horde

The *Frauen* are the leaders of the Wild Horde, the band of wandering souls, especially children's souls, who fly through the winter night skies (perhaps disguised as swans, or wild geese, or the wind). This is even true for St Lucy. In Norway, she is considered a loose woman, even a goblin, and is said to lead the Wild Hunt.

The Wild Horde itself was a complex phenomenon whose origins lose themselves partly in the prehistoric past. There was the assembly of ghosts under the leadership of a female divinity—Hecate or Artemis in ancient Greece; in the Latin West, Diana or Herodias, the mother of Salome. This gathering of female spirits, which later swelled into the crowd of evil hags at the witches' sabbath, was well known to theologians of the first millennium who in vain flung their anathema against it:

> As usual the effort was in vain. For as late as 1484 the Austrian Sephanius Lanzkranna reports in his *Hymmelstrasse* about the exploits of the Demon Dyana, whom he identifies with the local demons *frawe Percht* and *frawe Holt*. Herodias herself rides to the present day with the Wild Horde in large parts of Italy and in the eastern Alps... Ritual performances meant to

embody ghosts of the defunct—a feature not mentioned
by writers of the first millennium—have survived over a
large part of the eastern Alps under the name of Perchta,
a feminine demon in whom the spirit of the Carnival
is incarnated. [from Helen Farias]

Bernheimer, who wrote the long passage above, points out that
the masculine Wild Horde—led by Odin, Holler, Gwyn ap Nudd,
Herne the Hunter—is a more or less Teutonic phenomenon, while
the feminine one seems to be of Mediterranean origin.

In his book *Ecstasies,* in which he explores the imagery of the
witches' sabbath, Carlos Ginzburg describes evidence for an early
shamanic cult centered around a goddess of abundance and the
dead. She was known by many names: Herodiade, Diana, Ha-
bondia (Abundance), Richessa, and The Good Goddess (*Bona Dea,*
whose festival the Romans celebrated on December 1). Her devo-
tees said they flew with her through the night sky, entering the
houses of the rich to feast. Ginzburg suggests these journeys were
undertaken in trance.

Perchta was known to "eat food on the Table of Fortune."
There was a Roman Kalends (first of the month/year) or Saturnalia practice of laying tables with abundant food for some supernat-
ural being as a charm to ensure plenty for the coming year. It was
mentioned in the fifth century and also in the eleventh, when a
German ecclesiastical writer condemned the custom of putting out
food, drink, and three knives for "those three sisters whom the an-
cients in their folly called Parcae." The Parcae were the Roman
Fates, originally goddesses of abundance and motherhood (Parcae
derives from a word meaning to produce). In 1912, according to
Clement Miles, it was still the custom to lay out tables for "super-
natural beings, whether, as at All Souls' tide, explicitly for the dead,
or for Frau Perchta, or for the Virgin..."

Goddesses of Solstice

Our Lady of Solitude

Nuestra Senora de la Soledad

I fell in love with this particular manifestation of Mary when a friend brought me a postcard from Mexico depicting the statue of Our Lady of Solitude in the cathedral in Oaxaca. Her statue is dressed in black satin, ornamented with pearls and gold thread and lilies. Her pale, thin face shines like a silver moon in the star-spangled darkness of her clothing. I loved the idea of a goddess of solitude, especially so near the Winter Solstice.

She is the patron saint of the Lonely and also the patroness of Oaxaca and of sailor who bring her the pearls she wears in her crown. Processions are held in her honor for several nights previous to and on December 18, her feast day, with people carrying Japanese lanterns, candles, and figures of birds, a boat, banners displaying the sun and the moon, and other objects made of flowers, leaves, and colored paper. Offerings of nuts, fruits, and flowers are laid at Her feet.

Apparently, devotion to this compassionate aspect of Mary is common in Spanish-speaking cultures and honors Mary's silence and grief on Holy Saturday. The Church of Our Lady of Solitude in Oaxaca was built in 1692. Legend says that a mule driver, guiding his train of burros through Oaxaca, discovered that one of the animals was carrying a huge box, which when opened contained the image of the Blessed Virgin of Solitude. An enormous boulder at the entrance to the church marks the spot where the burro died from the weight of the box (perhaps this represents symbolically the burden of grief).

Virgin of Guadalupe

In 1531, on December 9, an indigenous farmer named Juan Diego was passing by the hill called Tepeyac outside of Mexico City on his way to an early morning mass when he heard birds singing overhead, with whistles, flutes, and beating wings. Then he saw a maiden dressed in the robes of an Aztec princess. She spoke Nahuatl, the Aztec language, Juan's language, and had skin as brown as cinnamon. She told Juan that she was Maria, the Mother of God, and that he should tell the Bishop of Mexico City to build her a chapel on the site. The bishop was not impressed by this message and demanded proof. The Virgin told Juan to climb the hill and gather an armful of Castilian roses, which should not have been blooming then. But when Juan opened his cloak to show the bishop the miraculous roses, he was surprised to see the bishop fall on his knees. On the cloak was an image of the virgin as she appeared to him, surrounded by an oval frame of stars. Of course, the chapel was built.

Our Lady of Guadalupe is affectionately known as *La Morenita*, the little dark one. The place on which she first appeared used to be a shrine to the ancient Aztec goddess, Tonantzin. According to Monaghan, Tonantzin was a mother-goddess honored on the Winter Solstice. She was portrayed by a woman dressed in white and covered with shells and eagle feathers, who danced through the crowd, weeping and singing, until she was ritually killed.

Yule Themes and Activities

Traditional Yule Themes

Battle between light and dark, the old year and the new year
Lighting lights in the darkness
Celebrating the rebirth of the Sun
Celebrating birth of the miraculous child
Welcoming the new year
Gathering with friends and family
Giving alms
Playing games, gambling
Reversing roles
Abstaining from normal tasks: no working!

Yule Activities

Take time off! Don't work!
Create or buy an Advent calendar
Create an Advent wreath
Create a creche or other shrine honoring
    the birth of the divine child (or the sun)
Light candles on the four Sundays before Christmas
Light candles—in the menorah, the kinara, on a Yule log
Decorate a festive Christmas candle
Decorate with evergreens, sparkling ornaments, and lights
Gather with friends and family
Eat a luxurious meal
Bake thirteen Christmas cookies or eat the Treize Desserts
Give gifts to children
Give gifts symbolic of the new year
Give to those less fortunate
Set out offerings for the birds
Wassail your trees
Play games or gamble

Yule Crafts

The Advent Wreath

Gertrud Mueller Nelson in *To Dance with God* talks about how people in the far north removed wheels from their carts during the depth of winter. They brought these wheels into their homes and decorated them with evergreens and candles. This, Nelson says, is the possible origin of the Advent wreath. Although a charming story, I suspect it was invented after the fact to explain the circular shape of the Advent wreath.

As far as I know, the Advent wreath began as a Catholic custom. An Advent wreath is a circle of evergreens with places for four candles: three violet for penance and one rose-colored (lit on the third week, which is called *Gaudete* [Rejoice] Sunday) to symbolize the coming joy. Nelson says in her family, they traditionally used red candles and red ribbon to decorate their wreath.

Helen Farias in *The Advent Sunwheel,* her book of suggestions for pagans wanting to celebrate Advent, points out that the Advent wreath, made of greens in a circle shape and lit by candles, is a potent symbol. The circle with the dot inside has long been a symbol for the sun, and is still used that way in astrology. Helen suggests putting a fifth candle in the center of the Advent wreath, to be lit on the solstice, to make the symbolism more apparent.

To make my Advent wreath on Wreath-Making Day, the Saturday before the first Sunday in Advent, I go on a walk through my neighborhood, collecting evergreen boughs. Often there's a big windstorm around this time that knocks off branches, so I don't have to cut them. When I do cut branches, since I will be using them with a spiritual intent, I always ask permission of the tree and leave an offering (usually cornmeal) at the base of the tree.

Many years ago, I bought a circular Styrofoam wreath form, which is the base for my Advent wreath. I hollowed out cavities just the width of standard candles, and I cover the Styrofoam with tin foil and then with evergreens, usually bound to the form with wire, ribbon, or ivy. I like to use candles in the colors of the four directions: yellow for east, red for south, blue for west, and green for north.

There is another kind of wreath, found in Germany and Scandinavia which is made of apples and dowels (chopsticks would work too). Three apples, with dowels connecting them in a triangle, form the base; the fourth apple is suspended by dowels above the rest, forming a pyramid. The triangle and pyramid are also sun symbols.

Marking Time

There are many ways of marking time during the darkest days of the year as we wait for the returning Light, from lighting candles on the menorah to setting up a creche.

Hungarians plant wheat seeds on St Lucy's Day (December 13). Kept in a warm room and watered daily, they are offered to the Infant in the manger on Christmas Day. In southern France, especially in Provence, the wheat grains are soaked in water, placed in dishes, and set to germinate in the warm chimney corner or a sunny window on St Barbara's day (December 4).

The grain is carefully tended, since if it grows fast, crops will do well in the coming year. Another folk divination performed on St Barbara's day is the gathering of cherry branches, which are brought into the house and placed in water. They bring good luck in the coming year if they bloom by the Solstice.

Advent Calendar

Several friends have made Advent calendars. Because I've seen firsthand the amount of time this takes, I prefer to buy mine in stores. There is something very magical about opening all those little doors and windows, even though I am often disappointed with the insipidity of the images. Isn't the mystery concealed almost always better than the thing revealed?

One of my friends, Carolee, made an Advent calendar with pictures cut from magazines. She used a beautiful landscape for the top layer and marked where to place the openings. She then found pictures that fit the openings (mostly birds, as I remember—she is an avid birder) and pasted them onto a backing sheet. Then she pasted the front picture to the back and created the doors with an X-Acto knife.

Another friend created an Advent calendar out of felt. The top half has a felt Christmas tree and the bottom half, numbered pockets, each containing a different charm. The charms are removed on the appropriate days and pinned to the Christmas tree.

Jesse Tree

The Jesse tree is a new custom developed as a Christian alternative to the Catholic (advent wreath) and pagan (Christmas trees) modes for marking time during the holy season. The Jesse tree is usually a branch (but it could be a potted plant), which is hung with ornaments representing different figures from the Old Testament or symbols referring to various Old Testament verses that prophesy the birth of Jesus—for instance, an ark for Noah, a burning bush for Moses, a harp for David, and so on.

Nativity Scene

Whether the focus is on the mother and child or on the divine hero, a central metaphor of Winter Solstice is birth. In Spanish, the Christmas greeting is "Feliz Navidad" ("Happy Birthday").

Representations of the Nativity are popular decorations in Christian households. When I was growing up, we set up the stable fairly early on in the Christmas season, and then add the various ceramic figures that appeared on the scene one by one, culminating in the placement of the Baby Jesus in the manger on Christmas morning. The Three Kings showed up somewhere around this time, over on one of the side tables, moving gradually closer to the stable (set up on top of the piano) until they also arrived on the scene on Epiphany.

In *To Dance with God*, Gertrud Mueller Nelson writes about the creche figures she inherited from her mother. Her mother made them while recovering from a serious illness out of bits of wire and pieces of cloth, and carved their hands and faces out of wood. Each figure, which could be moved and posed in many different ways, was thus imbued with her loving attention as well as tradition. My mother's nativity scene was a gift, given a few figures at a time, from my Aunt Jo and Uncle Bob, who bought unfinished clay figurines and painted them in brilliant colors.

Carol Field says that some Roman creches fill half a living room; new pieces are added over years, and they are set in specific landscapes, with representations of hills and trees, like elaborate train sets.

If the Christian imagery is not compatible with your spirituality, you can still create a nativity scene. Make a shrine to the sun that contains mirrors (long a sun symbol), a bowl of water, spiral designs, and items that sparkle and reflect. Since many of these are the same symbols that appear on my Christmas tree, you could also place ornaments on the tree one day at a time as a way of marking time. Or use the many types of modeling clay available today to make representations of Kore and Aeon, or Isis suckling Horus, or the Three Mothers.

John Matthews provides some great ideas for making a pagan shrine in his book *The Winter Solstice*—for instance, placing a figure of the Santa-shaman in a teepee of twigs surrounded by evergreen boughs and stones, or surrounding a candle (representing the sun) with statues of the animals of midwinter (the horse, the deer, the bear, the wren...).

Solstice Evergreen

Another ancient midwinter custom is decorating with greens. The Romans decorated with rosemary, bay, laurel, holly, ivy, and mistletoe. The holly and ivy were both important midwinter plants in Great Britain and Ireland, as seen in the mysterious medieval carol that mentions the rivalry between them. Matthews in *The Winter Solstice* provides the lyrics of a fifteenth century carol that refers to an ancient battle between the two, with the Ivy representing the cold gloominess of winter, and the Holly King representing the jolly spirit of the season.

The Christmas tree is of more recent origin. In her book *The Solstice Evergreen*, Sheryl Ann Karas says that the earliest record of an evergreen being decorated comes from Riga in Latvia in 1519, when a group of local merchants carried an evergreen bedecked with flowers to the marketplace, where they danced around it and then burned it. Another possible source is the custom in fifteenth and sixteenth century Germany of hanging apples on a fir tree as a prop for the miracle play performed on Christmas Eve that depicted Adam and Eve being driven out of Paradise.

Any kind of green can be used to make the Advent wreath, as described earlier. The wreath St Lucy wears is described variously as made out of green rue, lingonberries, whortleberry twigs, or bilberry twigs.

Other traditional Christmas greens include bay leaves and laurels (dating back to the Romans' celebration of Saturnalia), holly, ivy, and mistletoe. Wreaths made of evergreens like fir or pine are also welcome, because of their fragrance and the symbolism of their being evergreen, a sign of life in the darkness of winter.

Lloyd describes an English custom called the kissing bough, which preceded the Christmas tree. She says it was a garland or circle of greens, shaped in a double hoop and decorated with candles, colored paper, red apples, and ornaments with a bunch of mistletoe suspended from the center. It was hung in the middle of the ceiling of the main room, and the candles were lit for the first time on Christmas Eve and then every night for twelve nights.

Dee Hardie mentions colonial kissing balls, which she makes by making holes in a grapefruit with an icepick and then sticking in sprigs of boxwood, until the grapefruit looks like a "round green porcupine."

Gift-Giving and Games

The connection between Christmas and present-giving is fairly recent. In earlier times, people gave small symbolic gifts at Christmas time, such as gloves, pins, a coin, flowers, candy, a clove-studded orange, or sugar-coated figs. These were usually New Year's gifts, small tokens to wish luck or prosperity during the coming year.

Unfortunately, in twenty-first century America, spurred on by the advertising industry and the enormous boon for retail businesses, giving presents has become a major focus of the holiday season. All too often this practice becomes a burden, causing financial and emotional hardship.

The simplest way I've found to get off this Christmas gift-giving merry-go-round is to declare that I'm not buying any presents. Luckily my daughter was a somewhat cynical adolescent before I made this decision. The winter holidays have always been a time for honoring children, so a less radical choice might be to give gifts only to children.

My friend Candace offers to take each of her nieces and nephews on a special outing of their choice during December. She described the joy of her nine-year-old nephew when she took him to the candy store at the Seattle Center, then for a ride on the monorail to downtown, where he got to pet twenty-six horses (lined up on the street for holiday carriage rides), ride on the carousel, and visit another candy store where they got free samples. She took her twelve-year old niece to the mall, where they listened to CDs, tried on ball gowns, and ate junk food.

Several years ago, my daughter and I decided to make all of our Christmas gifts (we agreed that birthdays would be the time for store-purchased gifts). Since then, we've made and given each other a hand-painted silk scarf, a flannel nightgown, flannel sheets, a bracelet and earrings, a hand-painted ceramic mug, and a warm winter hat. One year, when she was visiting her dad for Christmas, I painted the walls of her room in colors she had chosen.

Although I stopped buying major presents for my daughter, I do fill her stocking with small gifts like gloves, socks, and an ornament. I also always give her a book to read and a game to play in those empty hours of Christmas afternoon. Besides making gifts for my daughter, I also make small token gifts for other people. One year I wrote stories about our pets, and Shaw illustrated them. We had them photocopied and bound into little books, which we distributed to close friends. Since then, the Christmas book has become a holiday tradition for me.

I don't always make a book each Christmas. Once I gave out handmade soap, and another year I made decorative tin lanterns. I have a friend who always makes a tape of his favorite music for the year, containing treasured bits of history, charting his evolving taste in music. Other friends give gifts of food: a loaf of pumpkin bread, a jar of chutney. Although these creative projects are probably more time-consuming than shopping, they are much more satisfying. It's a great way to withdraw your support from the consumer frenzy of the Christmas season, a mentality very far from the quiet, inward focus of winter.

Playing Snapdragon

I've celebrated Twelfth Night for many years, but it always seemed to lack a certain snap and sparkle despite all the ginger I put in the gingerbread. Finally, I discovered the missing ingredient: the game of snapdragon. Now it is also in great demand as the flaming conclusion to my annual Winter Solstice party.

I first heard about snapdragon (also known as flapdragon) while reading the *Annotated Alice*, where it is described as a Victorian Christmas game. The reference comes from *Through the Looking Glass*, where Alice meets the fanciful Looking-Glass insects. One of them is the snap-dragonfly, with a body made of plum-pudding, its wings of holly leaves, and its head a raisin burning in brandy. It lives on frumenty (a traditional Christmas porridge) and mince pie, and nests in a Christmas box.

This is how we play snapdragon at my house:

1. Fill a shallow heatproof bowl with raisins (or currants, if you want to make the game more difficult for your guests; I suggest raisins for your first attempt). Put in two or three raisins for each guest you think will participate.

2. Warm some brandy in a pan on the stove, then pour it into the bowl, about a half-inch deep.

3. Place the bowl in the middle of a table or on some other surface that can be protected from drips. We've always done this on a kitchen counter, but the floor around gets pretty messy. My friend Joanna covers a card table with tin foil, which makes an attractive reflective surface. I wouldn't want to try it over a wood floor or a pretty linen tablecloth.

4. Turn off as many lights as possible, for dramatic effect.

5. Light the brandy on fire. The brandy will flicker with an eerie blue flame.

6. Now try to snatch the raisins out of the burning brandy and pop them into your mouth.

Presumably, the person who eats the most wins—we've never played this competitively, but it might be a good way to choose the Twelfth Night King or Queen, since whoever is bold enough to succeed at this game is bound to have pretty interesting ideas for further merriment.

When you first see the flames, you will be convinced this cannot be done. Once you've decided to plunge your fingers into the burning brandy, there's the shock of discovering the flames are hot (but not hot enough to burn). If you persevere and snatch out a raisin, your fingers will drip with blue flame as you fling the still-burning raisin into your mouth. It's exciting and wild and daring and noisy—just the game to spice up a Twelfth Night party.

Luminarias

Every year I host a Winter Solstice party, and every year I like to send my guests home with a small handmade gift. One year, I found the perfect gift item in an issue of Martha Stewart's *Living*: luminarias made from tin cans. Although Martha featured this craft project in summer, I thought it was the perfect gift for Winter Solstice, with its symbolism of the returning light. It also resonated with the personal image I had been working with all that year: of letting my light shine, instead of hiding it.

The secret to making these lanterns is simple. Fill empty tin cans with water and put them in the freezer until the water is frozen. Then, use a hammer and nail to make designs in the sides. From making lanterns for all forty guests at my party, I learned some handy tips.

The best cans to use are condensed milk cans. In a year of collecting, these were the only cans I found that did not have corrugated sides. Although that's not too much of a problem when the lantern is in use, they aren't as attractive when the lights are on since the corrugations obscure the design.

To make the designs, brace the tin can against a towel, set the point of the nail where you want the hole to appear, and hammer away. The ice tends to chip away from the rim, so begin at the top and work your way down. But don't go too far. The biggest design flaw of my lanterns is that the wax leaks out the bottom holes when the candle burns down.

I invited friends over to help make the lanterns and enjoyed watching them come up with creative designs. I started with fairly repetitive patterns, like crosses, stars, flowers (one dot in the center surrounded by five other dots), and borders of staggered dots. But you can also make sun symbols (a circle around a dot), wave patterns, diagonal lines, vertical lines of varying lengths, or simply scatter random dots across the surface, like stars in space. You could write your name or the name of a friend. You can use a screwdriver and other wood-working tools to make more complicated patterns, especially if you are using large cans. But be careful: The heavier force of the screwdriver crumpled the sides of the flimsy tin cans I was using.

Also be careful when inserting candles into the lanterns. The inside edges are very sharp. For the same reason, be cautious about giving these to small children. I own a beautiful decorative tin lantern from Mexico, made from a sheet of tin pierced while laying flat, then bent into a circle, and fitted onto a base. When made this way, the sharp edges are all on the outside, making it easier to insert and light a candle.

My house was beautiful last Winter Solstice, glowing with these little tin lanterns. There were many left after the guests departed with their chosen lanterns. These have been put to good use all year long. I light one on my desk when I'm writing. A few found a place on the bathroom counter, for candlelight baths. A few more garnish the piano and ornament my altar. The rest are packed away in the Christmas box. I look forward each year to setting them out and seeing how the house is transformed by the flickering light, like the sparkle of hundreds of stars, of my Winter Solstice luminarias.

Pomanders

Golden Apples of the Sun

Were you ever disappointed as a child when you found that the heavy lump at the bottom of your Christmas stocking was just an orange? I was. But it turns out this symbol of good luck and abundance might be one of the oldest of Christmas traditions.

The word pomander comes from *pomme* (meaning apple, also the root of Pomona, the Roman goddess of fruits) and *arbre* (amber or golden in color). I like to translate pomander as golden apples. The golden ball of dominion is also a *pomme*, as in the pommel of a sword, on which people swore; and three golden balls are the emblem of St Nicholas (later Santa Claus).

Pomanders are very old; they are mentioned in the *Romance of the Rose* in 1280. Around Elizabethan times, noblefolk had pomanders shaped like apples and oranges but made out of gold, silver, ivory, or china, often encrusted with jewels and powdered gold, and packed with aromatic mixtures. The scents were supposed to ward off disease. They hung on a chain around one's neck or waist. Queen Elizabeth always wore one. Cardinal Wolsey carried a cheaper version, a hollowed orange or apple filled with spices.

In the seventeenth and eighteenth centuries, many authors mention the decorated orange stuck with cloves. In the Christmas masque of Ben Jonson: "He has an Orange and rosemary, but not a clove to stick in it." Brand mentions children going around at New Year's carrying pippins and oranges stuck with cloves to crave a blessing for their godparents.

Pomanders are traditional New Year's gifts. In Scotland, people give and receive Hogmanays, an apple stuck with cloves and rosemary (or holly). Carol Field says that in Italy it is traditional to give lentils, raisins, and oranges on New Year's Day as symbols of riches, good luck, and the promise of life. The Romans gave each other gifts on New Year's Day: little dolls of clay and palm, or bay branches hung with sweets, dates, figs, and gilded fruits. Oranges are also given as gifts at Chinese New Year as a symbol of good fortune.

In Wales, the Calennig, the New Year apple, is studded with wheat, oats, nuts, and raisins, then powdered with wheat flour and touched in gold leaf. Sprigs of box and rosemary are stuck on top, and half-cracked hazel nuts attached to the ends of the leaves so the shells clasp the foliage. It is placed on a tripod of holly or rowan skewers; a fourth skewer is used for a handle. This decorated apple is found in Monmouth, Glamorgan, and Carmarthen while in other districts they use an orange.

Making Pomanders

You can make a pomander using oranges, apples, lemons, or limes. Andy Van Hevlingen, who provides instructions on making pomanders for *The Herb Companion*, likes to use small smooth-skinned tangerines. He looks for fruits with an attached stem so he can tie a ribbon around it.

Prick holes with an ice pick or a large needle, then stud the surface evenly and closely with cloves. Van Hevlingen suggests that if you sort your pile of cloves into two piles, one with heads and one without; you can use these to make patterns. If you are going to keep the pomander for a long time, cover the surface completely. If you are just going to float it in the Yule punch, you can experiment with designs.

When done, place the pomanders on newspapers in a well-ventilated location and turn them daily. In a heated house, they will usually dry within a week or so. Some pomander makers suggest rolling the hardened pomander in a mixture of equal parts of powdered orris root* with cinnamon or allspice (about ½ tablespoon per fruit), and then turning it daily. I tried this, and so did Van Hevlingen; neither of us liked the results, because it muddled the pattern. Perhaps pomanders were originally rolled in flour like the Calennig as a charm for abundance.

Pomanders can be floated in a Yule punch, kept in a drawer for sweet scent, displayed as a centerpiece on the table, hung on a tree for decoration (Dee Hardie decorates her kitchen tree with clove-studded oranges, lemons, and limes) or put in the toe of a stocking to continue the tradition.

* Warning! Orris root causes severe allergic reactions in some people.

Celebrating with Food

Christmas Porridge

A special porridge is traditional fare in many countries during the winter season. Sometimes it is connected with the legend of a winter saint and the miraculous appearance of grain during a famine. Try one of these recipes (all from Mimi Sheraton's book *Visions of Sugar Plums*) on Solstice Eve, or perhaps for a festive Christmas morning breakfast.

Kahmie for St Barbara

In the Levant, this is the traditional dish for St Barbara's day (December 4). The legend of St Barbara is told while the *kahmie* is cooking.

> 3 cups whole grain wheat*
> 1 t salt
> 1 cup golden raisins
> ½ cup chopped blanched walnuts
> ½ cup blanched halved almonds
> ½ cup pine nuts
> 1 cup sugar (or ½ cup sugar and 1/3 cup honey)
> 3 to 4 drops of rose water
> 3 to 4 drops orange flower water
> cinnamon
> sugar
> chopped walnuts, almonds, or pistachios
> * Soaking the grain overnight will cut cooking time.

Wash the grain thoroughly in boiling water. Drain well and place in a heavy saucepan with 8 cups of boiling water. Cover tightly and simmer slowly until the grain is completely tender— between 4 and 6 hours if not pre-soaked. Add more boiling water if necessary.

Toward the end of the cooking time, stir in just enough salt to eliminate the watery flavor. Cook to a porridge consistency, with all the water absorbed by the time the grain is done. Drain off any excess water.

Over low heat, stir in the raisins, pine nuts, walnuts, almonds, sugar/honey, and flavored waters. Stir until all the sugar is dissolved and the mixture is thick and moist.

Remove from the heat, turn into individual custard cups or dessert dishes or one large serving bowl, and chill thoroughly. Stir and serve sprinkled with cinnamon, sugar, and chopped nuts. Makes 8 to 10 servings.

Kutya for Father Frost

In the Ukraine, *kutya* is left outside for "Father Frost" to keep him from freezing the crops later in the year. A portion is also thrown to the ceiling—the number of grains that stick indicate how many bees you'll have in your hive the next year. A spoon is left in the remaining porridge overnight, so the spirits of the dead ancestors can help themselves (likely the origin of the custom of leaving out food for Santa).

Cook wheat as above. Mix with 2 to 3 cups of honey, and simmer 5 to 10 minutes. Stir in ½ cup blanched, dried, and ground poppy seeds, and chill. If you wish, you can add ¼ cup sweet cream to the poppy seeds before stirring them into the wheat. Sprinkle with chopped almonds or walnuts before serving.

Armenian Anoush Abour

Make just the same as *kahmie,* but when stirring in the raisins and nuts, also add 10 to 12 dried apricots cut into quarters, and omit the orange water.

Cuccia for Lucia

When St Lucy sent a flotilla of grain ships to the harbor at Palermo (or Syracuse—the location is hotly contested between the two cities) on December 11 in 1582, the people were so hungry they couldn't wait to grind the wheat and so ate it whole, which is why Sicilians don't eat anything made with wheat flour on St Lucy's day.

The dish *cuccia* (conveniently rhymes with Lucia) is Arabic; the word is dialect for wheat berries or grains. Carol Field (who provides this recipe in *Celebrating Italy*) points out that the grains, like seeds, hold the promise of abundance at the next harvest. Peasant women looked for traces of the saint's passing in the pan where the *cuccia* was cooked.

> 1 pound plus 2 oz. soft white wheat berries
> 1 pinch salt
> 2 pounds 2 oz. fresh ricotta
> (or 2 pounds fresh ricotta and 2 oz. goat cheese)
> 1-¼ cups sugar
> ¼ t vanilla extract
> 1/3 cup candied orange peel or citron
> A few chocolate chips

Begin soaking the wheat berries three days before you plan to serve the *cuccia*; cover them with water and change the water twice a day. On the fourth day, drain the berries and place them in a large pot. Cover with lightly salted water, bring to a boil, and simmer over the lowest possible flame until soft and almost bursting, about 3 to 6 hours. Remove from the fire, cover with a lid, and let them stand 6 to 8 hours.

Meanwhile, press the ricotta through a sieve into a mixing bowl and stir well. Add the sugar and vanilla, and beat until creamy. Let the mixture sit at least 2 hours, then press through a sieve again.

Drain the wheat berries extremely well, squeezing out all the excess water, and add them to the ricotta cream. Stir in the orange peel or citron. Serve in little cups or bowls as they do in the streets and in the houses of Palermo, with a few shavings of chocolate or tiny chocolate chips on top.

Julerisengrod (Danish Rice Porridge)

The Danes leave some of this porridge in front of each door or in the attic on Christmas Eve for the *Julenissen*, the Yuletide elves who watch over animals, especially cats. It should contain one almond, a token of good luck for the person who finds it.

> 2 cups long-grained rice
> 1-½ quarts whole milk

1 whole almond
½ cup heavy cream
½ t salt
butter, cinnamon, and sugar

Scald rice with boiling water. Drain and repeat with fresh boiling water. Heat milk in the top of a double boiler. When simmering, stir in rice gradually so the milk doesn't stop cooking. Stir with a wooden spoon until the milk boils.

Reduce heat, cover, and cook the rice slowly until very soft, about 1 to 1-½ hours, stirring occasionally to prevent scorching. Remove from the heat and stir in the almond, cream, and salt. Serve in warm cereal or soup bowls. Garnish each portion with butter, cinnamon, and sugar.

Christmas Dinner

Christmas dinner is one of those grand seasonal feasts for which each culture has its own set of traditional dishes. In France, the big meal, called the *revillon* (meaning the beginning of a new watch), is served immediately after midnight mass. It often begins with oysters and champagne. Roast turkey with chestnuts is the usual dish, but in former times, each region had its own specialty: a *daube* (beef in red wine) in Armagnac; sauerkraut and goose liver in Alsace; *aligot* in Auvergne; black pudding (blood sausage) in Nivernais; and goose in southwestern France. In the southeast, a large meal was eaten before mass consisting of cauliflower and salt cod (perhaps with snails), grey mullet with olives, or omelet with artichokes and fresh pasta.

The Germans serve goose with apples, prunes, and sweet-and-sour red cabbage. Red cabbage is also traditional in Spain. The Basque Christmas dinner has three courses: vegetables, then red bream, and finally a stuffed turkey or capon or a fried steak. The Poles eat foods containing poppy seeds. Romans eat eels. In Bologna, it's tortellini stuffed with minced ground pork, turkey, sausage, cheese, and nutmeg, followed by desserts of *nocciata* (walnuts and honey, cut into triangles), *cassata* flavored with ricotta cheese and chocolate, and *torrone*, made with almonds.

Sicilians serve a meatless meal of seven fish on Christmas Eve. Loosee, writing an article on this custom for Christmas.com, says that it was customary to visit seven churches on Christmas Eve, before the evening meal of seven fish. Her grandmother served *baccala* (cod), calamari, fish salad, a special Christmas sauce made with smelt and eel (she's added crab and shrimp). Eating fish cleansed and prepared people for the indulgence in meat dishes on Christmas Day. Marian Scotto, part-owner of Fresco, an Italian restaurant in New York City, serves a Christmas Eve dinner that begins with a hearty seafood salad (with shrimp, calamari, crabmeat, and scallops), followed by crab cakes, spaghetti with lobster ragout, and herb-grilled tuna.

The Germans used to serve "blue carp," a fish that had been specially fattened for Christmas from August onwards, turned blue by pouring hot vinegar over it before cooking, and served with sour cream, horseradish, and apples. Now the main dish is more likely to be goose, turkey, venison, wild boar, or a roast. However, apples, walnuts, and almonds are always served.

The Swedes for centuries have feasted on marinated lingcod, served in a white sauce with butter, potatoes, mustard, and black pepper. The Danes like roast goose stuffed with apples and prunes and garnished with red cabbage, caramelized potatoes, and cranberry sauce. Dessert consists of rice porridge or rice with almonds and cherry compote. The Norwegians serve roast pork chops and sauerkraut (flavored with cumin). The Finns cook a ham in a rye-flour pastry case. In all the Scandinavian countries, Christmas is the occasion for a sumptuous smorgasbord.

Wigilia

The Poles celebrate Christmas Eve, or the Vigil of Christmas, with a special feast that begins when the first star is seen. Hay is placed beneath the tablecloth, and a candle is lit in the window to light the way for the Christ Child. Sheaves of grain stand in the corners of the room, to symbolize the wish for a good harvest. There should be an even number of diners and an odd number of dishes. The feast begins with each family member breaking a piece from the *oplatek*, a large unleavened piece of bread that has been stamped with scenes of the Nativity.

As in Sicily, this meal contains no meat. The special dishes include mushrooms, carp, and *kutya*, a wheat pudding that is often served but seldom eaten. Dessert includes a compote of twelve stewed fruits, in honor of the Apostles. Presents are opened after the meal and before midnight mass.

Horst Scharfenberg, in *Cuisines of Germany*, publishes this menu as typical for a Polish Wigilia:

Blini Mushrooms in Sour Cream Borscht
Pike with Hot Horseradish Sauce
Bohemian Christmas Carp
Noodles with Poppy Seeds
Beans with Plums
Sauerkraut
Vareniki (dumpling)
Medivnyk (honey cake)
Compote of Stewed Fruits
Vodka
Coffee

Christmas Desserts

Most countries also have a traditional Christmas cake. In France, it's *buche de noel*, a cake of dough rolled up and frosted with buttercream to look like a log. In England it's a fruitcake, often soaked in alcohol, and then spread with apricot jam, almond paste, and frosting. In Germany, it's *stollen*, which contains crystallized fruit. In Alsace, it's *bireweck* (a cake that includes nuts and dried and candied fruit) served with compotes and gingerbread, traditionally eaten before midnight mass. In Brittany, it's a star-shaped *fouace*.

In France, the dinner concludes with the traditional Thirteen Desserts. Each one must be tasted to bring good luck in the coming year. According to *Larousse Gastronomique*, the number thirteen commemorates the thirteen participants at the Last Supper (however, this seems a bit far-fetched and out-of-season as well). The desserts are: *pompe a l'huile* (a fruit pastry), raisins, quince paste, marzipan sweets, nougat, *fougasse* (a rich cake), walnuts and hazelnuts, crystallized (candied) citrons, winter pears, Brignoles plums, dried figs, almonds, and dates. Carol Field describes a similar tradition in regions of Italy that were once part of Magna Grecia (reinforcing my belief that the number thirteen is more ancient than the Last Supper), where thirteen kinds of fruits and nuts are served at the end of the Christmas Eve meal, including nuts, figs, olives, melon, and mandarin oranges.

Thirteen Cookies

My friend and colleague Helen Farias first told me that you should bake thirteen different kinds of cookies during the Christmas season. Although I've been searching for years, I've never found a source that mentions thirteen cookies. Perhaps she got this idea from the tradition of the Thirteen Desserts. My goal is to make three batches of cookies during each of the four weeks of Advent, and one extra batch during the final week, so I can serve thirteen kinds of cookies at my Winter Solstice party.

Bolo De Mel

Portuguese women begin baking the *bolo de mel* cake on December 8, will be eaten on Epiphany (January 6), the feast of Mary's Immaculate Conception. This honey cake (now usually sweetened with molasses) is dense with walnuts, almonds, and candied peel. It is traditional to leaven the cake with a piece of dough from bread-baking. Also, any honey cakes left from the previous year must be eaten before the new one is made. The cake is made in the shape of a ring. Besides the dried lima bean (which designates the King, who must make the cake the following year), the cake also contains amulets and fortune-telling trinkets.

The following recipe comes direct from a Portuguese woman in Madeira via the website Recipe Cottage: This is a traditional recipe from the days before every house had an oven, when the cake was baked in the village's huge common oven. I've kept the directions as close to the original as possible. I think it gives you a good idea of how to make an authentic *bolo de mel* cake, which you can adapt if you like.

> 9 ounces (250 g) bread dough from the baker's shop
> 1 cup Madeira wine
> 5 Tablespoons bicarbonate of soda, dissolved in the Madeira wine
> 60 ounces (1.8 lt) pure honey
> 26 ounces (750 g) *banha* (pork fat; or substitute butter)

17 ounces (500 g) butter
90 ounces (2.5 kg) flour
35 ounces (1 kg) sugar
1 ounce (25 g) *erva-doce* (anise herbs, mashed and sifted)
1.75 ounce (50 g) *canela* (cinnamon)
1 ounce (25 g) *cravinho da india* (cloves in powder form)
1.75 ounce (50 g) candied lemon peel, cut into cubes
4 oranges (scrape the skin and keep, then get the juice)
17 ounces (500 g) walnut, cut into halves
9 ounces (250 g) ground almonds

One day before making the cake, buy the bread dough at the baker's shop, pat a little bit of flour on the dough, put it in a towel, and keep it in a warm place until next day. Put the bicarbonate of soda into the Madeira, dissolve. In a pan, warm up the honey, add the butter and pork fat, and let cool. Sift flour into a bowl, add the sugar, then create a crater in the middle, and put the bread dough in the middle. Work the flour-sugar-mixture into the bread dough.

As soon as this is well combined, incorporate little by little the honey-fat-mixture. To the dough, add most of the candied lemon peel, the cup of Madeira wine, orange juice, the scraped orange skin, anise, cinnamon, cloves. Incorporate and knead thoroughly until the dough no longer sticks on the bowl. Cover the dough with a towel and keep it in a warm place for 3 to 4 days.

Divide the dough into parts of 250 g or 500 g or 750 g, depending on the size of pan you are planning to use. This cake is made in wide, round, low pans. Grease the pan. Decorate the top with halved walnuts, sliced almonds, and the rest of the candied lemon peel.

Bake about 50 minutes at 355F (180C). Let cool before taking out of the pan.

Twelfth Night Cake

Throughout Europe, a special cake is served on Twelfth Night, the end of the Twelve Days of Christmas and the winter holidays. In England, a bean and a pea are baked into the cake (I've used spice gumdrops), and whoever received the portion with the bean becomes the Twelfth Night King, while the person with the pea becomes the

Queen. You can play it this way, with genders unessential, or the old-fashioned way: if a woman gets the bean, she chooses the King, and vice versa for the pea.

The royal pair assigns titles to the rest of the company as they wish, thus creating a mock court. Since this is an opportunity to make fun of existing institutions, you may want to assign political titles or dysfunctional family roles instead. In France, every move the Twelfth Night royal couple makes is commented on and imitated with mock ceremony. For instance: "The Queen drinks!" "The King sneezes!" In my house, the King or Queen gets to order the others around, with an emphasis on making them do silly and uncharacteristic things.

This Twelfth Night Cake from Spicer's book, *From an English Oven*, makes a sort of fruitcake. Since I don't like fruitcake, I usually serve a batch of ginger snaps (one for each guest) on a platter with one marked with a special design on the top or a bit of frosting on the bottom. The person choosing the cookie becomes the Queen; if no one chooses it, then I become the Queen. We always crown the Queen with a gold foil wreath and hand her a scepter. We also rotate the position (with a new batch of cookies), since people tire of the role of ringmaster.

> 3 cups sifted flour
> 1 Tbsp molasses
> 3/8 cup currants
> 3 eggs
> ¾ cup sultanas
> ¼ cup milk
> 1-1/3 cups mixed peel, shredded
> ¼ tsp allspice
> 1 cup butter
> 1-¼ tsp cinnamon
> 5/8 cup brown sugar

Cream together butter and sugar. Add the eggs, one at a time, beating thoroughly after each addition. Warm the molasses and milk, and add them to the butter, sugar, and eggs, beating briskly. Sift a little of the flour over the fruits, to prevent them from falling to the bottom of the pan. Stir together flour and spices, and mix into the batter, stirring lightly. Fold in the fruits last of all.

Line a bread tin with waxed paper. Pour in this mixture and bake in a slow oven (250 F) for approximately 2 to 2-¼ hours.

Galette des Rois

In France, the special cake served on Twelfth Night is the *galette des rois*. It is thin and round, and is cut into pieces in the pantry, always one more piece than there are guests, and carried into the room covered with a white napkin. The youngest member of the party gets to distribute the pieces. A small china doll (formerly a bean) is baked into the cake, and the person receiving this piece becomes the Queen or King and gets to choose a consort. The extra piece is called *le part a Dieu,* and is set aside for the first person to come through the door. This recipe is adapted from Marilyn Bright's *The Christmas Cookbook.*

> 1 lb prepared puff pastry
> ½ cup fine sugar
> ½ cup butter
> ½ cup ground almonds
> 2 egg yolks
> a few drops almond extract
> 1 T rum
> beaten egg white

Divide the pastry in half and roll it into two rounds, about 10 inches across. Cream together the sugar and butter until light and fluffy. Then work in the egg yolks, almonds, almond extract, and rum. Spread the filling on one of the rounds. If you want to add a token (pea or bean) for the Twelfth Night King or Queen, add it now.

Moisten the edges of the pastry, and cover it with the second round, pressing the edges to seal. With the point of a knife, score with wavy lines radiating from the center of the pastry or with a simple lattice pattern. Brush with some of the beaten egg white, and bake in a preheated oven at 375F for about 30 minutes, or until the pastry is golden brown. Serve warm.

Christmas Beverages

Almost all holiday beverages are spicy and served warm (except egg-nog, which must be served cold because of the raw eggs it contains, but its warm yellow color represents the sun). They also usually contain alcohol to further warm the body and the spirits. Besides the recipes here, you might consider hot buttered rum and Irish coffee.

Bishop's Wine

The traditional drink served in the Netherlands on this holiday is a mulled wine called Bishop's Wine. I am not sure if this is the sort of wine enjoyed by bishops, once renowned for their sensual indulgences and luxuries, or because it's associated with St Nicholas, who was the Bishop of Myra.

To make Bishop's Wine, stud an orange with cloves (some recipes also have you do this to a lemon). Pour a bottle of dry red wine (or claret) into a saucepan (or into a crockpot, which you can use to keep it warm all night), add the clove-studded orange (and lemon) and some cinnamon sticks. Simmer the wine until it is permeated with the flavors of the spices. Add sugar to taste. Serve hot.

Julglogg: Flaming Punch

> 1 bottle red Bordeaux-style wine
> 2 slices fresh ginger
> 2 sticks cinnamon
> ½ teaspoon cardamom seeds
> 6 to 8 cloves
> ¼ cup sugar cubes
> 1/3 cup schnapps (or vodka)
> 1/3 cup raisins
> 2 tbsp blanched almonds

Simmer the wine, ginger, and spices in a saucepan until the flavor of the spices permeates the wine. You can do this ahead of time and set the wine aside for several hours. When ready to serve, heat the spiced wine until it is almost boiling. Meanwhile, heat the schnapps separately.

Pour the glogg into a punch bowl, and put a metal grate over the bowl. Moisten the sugar cubes with a little of the hot schnapps, and place on the grate. Ignite the remaining schnapps, and pour over the sugar cubes until they have completely melted into the glogg. Put the raisins and almonds in mugs, and ladle in the hot glogg.

Wassail

Wassail was originally a drink of spiced ale with bits of toast (hence our term "toasting") or whole apples floating on top. The apple was the last harvest of the year, and wassail is the drink of this season, from Halloween through Yule, perhaps because the apple is associated with the Celtic Underworld and this is the time of death in the natural world.

Wassailing refers to both the custom of going around singing carols and expecting to be invited in for strong drink and food, and the custom of pouring a libation to the apple trees, to thank them for the past harvest and ensure a good harvest in the year to come.

> 1 quart ale
> 1 t cinnamon
> 5 to 6 pieces cracked ginger or 1 t powdered
> 2 cups sherry wine
> juice and zest of 1 lemon
> sugar to taste
> 2 slices toasted bread
> 6 to 8 roasted crab apples or 2 to 3 large apples

Heat ale in an enameled saucepan until it is just below the boiling point. Stir in spices, sherry, lemon juice, zest, and sugar. Stir until the sugar dissolves, then cover, and steep over low heat for 20 to 30 minutes. Never boil!

Pour into heated bunch bowl. Add toast and apples. Ladle into warm punch cups. Makes about 12 servings.

Variations:

♦ Add thirteen small well-beaten eggs to the hot wassail before adding the apples.

♦ Use brown sugar and beer instead of white sugar and ale.

♦ Or use hard cider in place of ale, or use 1 cup dark rum for the sherry.

♦ For a non-alcoholic version, replace the ale and sherry with sweet apple cider.

Eggnog

This recipe, which serves thirty, comes from John Matthew's book *The Winter Solstice.*

> 12 eggs
> 1-½ cups (12 oz.; 350 g) sugar
> 1 quart (1.1 lt) heavy cream
> 1 quart (1.1 lt) milk
> 1 quart (1.1 lt) bourbon (or scotch or rum)
> 1 cup (8 oz.; 250 ml) rum

This should be made about a week before serving to allow it to mellow. Separate the eggs. Beat the egg whites together until stiff, then beat in ½ cup (4 oz.; 100 g) of sugar. Beat the egg yolks until pale and light. Add the remaining sugar and ¼ teaspoon of salt. Combine the egg mixture with the milk and bourbon. Beat well, then add the rum. Pour into a jug and store in a cool place.

Shake or stir thoroughly before serving. Sprinkle with nutmeg, if desired.

Hanukkah Treats

Hanukkah foods tend to be cooked in oil, like potato latkes and doughnuts, thus connecting the holiday feast with the historical legend about the ever-replenishing oil for the lamps of the Temple.

Sfeenj (Orange Doughnuts)

This recipe comes from Elizabeth Luard, who says these doughnuts are eaten in Morocco to celebrate Hanukkah. She recommends putting some in a basket, going out to the street, and handing them to passersby, to fulfill your holiday duty of giving alms.

> 4 cups bread flour
> 1 t salt
> 2 t dry yeast
> 3 T sugar
> 3 medium eggs, lightly whisked
> ½ cup orange juice
> grated zest of 1 orange

3 T vegetable oil
plus oil for frying
powdered sugar
finely grated orange zest

Start with all the ingredients at room temperature. Combine flour, salt, yeast, and sugar. Make a well in the middle of the flour, and pour in the eggs, orange juice, zest, and oil. Knead until the dough is soft and pliable but no longer sticky (add flour or water if necessary). Work into a ball. Rub the dough surface slightly with oil, and drop it back into the bowl.

Cover and let rise until doubled, at least one hour (rich dough like this takes longer to rise than regular dough). Punch down the dough with your fist, then form it into a rope. Cut into twenty pieces and roll each into a ball. Transfer to a floured tray and set in a warm place to rise another hour, until again doubled in bulk.

Heat just enough frying oil to submerge doughnuts. As soon as the oil is very hot, slip in a few balls of dough at a time. Fry, flipping once, until golden brown and well-risen. Remove and drain on paper towels. Finish with a dusting of powdered sugar and grated orange zest.

Latkes

This recipe comes from Joan Nathan's *Jewish Holiday Kitchen*. She traces the history of latkes from Jews living in the Ukraine whose Christian neighbors served potato pancakes along with their goose for Christmas. The original latkes were made from grated potatoes cooked in goose oil. Now there are many recipes for latkes, which might have apples, zucchini, carrots, parsley, or onions added to the recipe.

10 medium potatoes
2 medium onions
2 large or 3 medium eggs
¼ cup unbleached flour, breadcrumbs, or matzah meal
salt and pepper to taste
vegetable oil

Peel the potatoes if the skin is coarse; otherwise, simply scrubbing them is fine. Keep them in cold water until you are ready. Grate some onion on the large holes of the grater and potatoes on the smallest holes. This will help keep the potatoes from blackening. Press out as much liquid as possible, and reserve the starchy sediment at the bottom of the bowl. You can also use the steel blade (for a smooth texture) or grating blade (for a crunchy texture) of a food processor to grate the potatoes and onions. Blend the potato mixture and the sediment with the eggs, flour, and salt and pepper.

Heat one inch of oil in a frying pan. For each latke, drop about 1 Tablespoon of the mixture into the skillet and fry, turning once. When golden and crisp on each side, drain on paper towels. Serve with yogurt, sour cream, sugar, or applesauce.

You can freeze latkes after making them, if you place them on a cookie sheet and put it in the freezer, then store in a plastic bag. Reheat in a 450F oven for several minutes. But don't store them in the refrigerator—they'll become soggy.

Carols and Poems

Welcome Yule!

This beautiful poem by Susan Cooper is usually the culminating moment of any Revels performance. It gives me chills down my back every time I read it.

> So the shortest day came, and the year died,
> and everywhere down the centuries
> of the snow-white world
> came people singing, dancing
> to drive the dark away.
> They lighted candles in the winter trees,
> They hung their homes with evergreens;
> They burned beseeching fires all night long
> to keep the year alive.
> And when the new year's sunshine blazed awake
> they shouted, reveling,
> through all the frosty ages you can hear them
> echoing, behind us—listen!
> All the long echoes sing the same delight,
> this shortest day,
> as promise wakens in the sleeping land:
> they carol, feast, give thanks,
> and dearly love their friends, and hope for peace.
> And so do we, here, now,
> this year, and every year.
> Welcome Yule!

Twelfth Night

> Now, now the mirth comes
> With the cake full of plums,
> Where Bean's the King of the sport here;

Besides we must know,
The Pea also
Must revel, as Queen, in the Court here.
Begin then to choose
This night as you use
Who shall for the present delight here,
Be a King by the lot,
and who shall not
Be Twelfth-day Queen for the night here.
Which known, let us make
Joy-sops with the cake,
And let not a man be seen here,
Who unurg'd will not drink
To the base from the brink
A health to the King and Queen here.
Next crown the bowl full
With gentle lamb's wool;
Add sugar, nutmeg and ginger,
With store of ale too;
And this you must do
To make the wassail a swinger.
— Robert Herrick

Santa Lucia

The radiant light-bringing goddess still appears in the darkness of
the winter, bearing the gift of light and food in her hands, even if
she is now known as Saint Lucy or Santa Lucia instead of Juno Lucina
or Freya. This song is sung to the tune of the traditional Neapolitan
song of the same name.

The lyrics are by Arvid Rosen, and the translation is a bit awkward in places:

> Night plods with heavy trend, court and cot cov'ring
> O'er earth, now sunshine's sped. Shadows are hov'ring
> Mirk in our home takes flight.
> When comes with tapers bright
> Sancta Lucia, Sancto Lucia, Sancta Lucia.

If the traditional lyrics seem too stiff for you, you might like this version, written by my daughter, Shaw:

> Darkness is at its peak
> But light is on its way.
> Springtime is coming soon,
> Winter will fade away.
> She brings light to our house.
> She brings joy to our lives.
> Santa Lucia, Santa Lucia.

Deck the Halls

This classic Welsh carol is also a New Year's carol, and one that celebrates the flaming Yule log. The lyric about following in merry measure also suggests the origin of all carols—they were originally meant to be danced. Although I don't know of any particular dance steps that go with this carol or any others, but you might try inventing a round or contra dance, to fit the lyrics.

Deck the halls with boughs of holly
Fa la la la la la la la la!
'Tis the season to be jolly Fa la la la...!
Don we now our gay apparel Fa la la la...!
Troll the ancient Yuletide carol Fa la la la...!
See the blazing Yule before us Fa la la la...!
Strike the harp and join the chorus Fa la la la...!
Follow me in merry measure Fa la la la...!
While I tell of Yuletide treasure Fa la la la...!
Far away the old year passes, Fa la la la...!
Hail the new, ye lads and lasses Fa la la la...!
Sing we joyous all together Fa la la la...!
Heedless of the wind and weather Fa la la la...!

The Boar's Head Carol

Like "Deck the Halls," this medieval carol seems to predate Christianity (especially if you understand the reference to Lord applying to the lord of the household). It is sung while carrying in the boar's head, the prime dish of the Midwinter feast.

The pig is the sacred animal of the Goddess. It was a frequent offering to Demeter, and the boar was particularly sacred to Freya, the Norse Queen of Heaven. On New Year's Eve in Vienna, pigs are let loose at midnight in crowded restaurants, and all the patrons scramble to touch the pig to garner good luck for the coming year. In private homes, a substitute is a marzipan pig suspended from the ceiling with a gold piece in its mouth

The Latin translated:

> *Quod estis in convivio* (As you are in good company)
> *Caput apri defero* (The boar's head we bring)
> *Reddens laudes Domino* (Giving praises to the Lord)
> *Servire cantico* (Serve it singing)
> *In Teginensi atrio* (In the Queen's Hall) [from Oxford]

Carol of the Bells

One of my favorite Christmas carols is the Ukrainian *Carol of the Bells*, also known as *Ring Silver Bells*. I was happy to learn more about it from the program notes of the Seattle Men's Chorus 1992 Christmas performance. It's not really a Christmas carol, but rather a New Year's carol or *Schedriwka*. It was sung on *Schedrij Vechir*, Epiphany, or New Year's Eve by roving bands of carolers who dressed in costumes and went looking for handouts (like Halloween trick-or-treaters, or wassailers, or the folks that personified the spirits of the dead between the old year and the new year). The word *Schedrij* refers to abundance and prosperity. Thus, *Schedriwka* express wishes for material blessings in the New Year.

Here is a translation of the original Ukrainian text, translated by Olga Zachary, of St Nicholas the Wonderworker Ukrainian Catholic Church in Victoria B.C., and Reverend Kenneth Olson, the pastor of the parish. The (anonymous) writer of the program notes apologizes for the disparaging remarks about women, but I take it to be playful teasing, the sort of bantering remarks you indulge in with your co-workers or best friends.

> On new year!
> The bird of bounty, the swallow,
> arrives this evening
> and she begins her sweet singing,
> calling out to the master of the house:
> "Come out, come out, Master of this house,
> and look upon your flocks.
> See your fat ewes rolling over
> and giving birth to healthy lambs."
> This flock of yours is a first-class flock;
> it will bring you lots of cash.
> Not so your dark-browed wife.
> She'll bring no cash.
> She's more like chaff,
> this woman of dark eyebrows.

A New Year Carol

This song appears in *Come Hither*, a collection of verse edited by Walter de la Mare. It appears to be a traditional folk text. Benjamin Britten put the poem to music in 1936. This arrangement for four-part harmony was created by Elena Richmond, who changed the first verse slightly.

Trefor Owen describes the context for this song in Wales. Very early on New Year's Day, about three or four o'clock in the morning, groups of boys came round to the houses in the neighborhood, carrying a vessel of cold spring water, freshly drawn, and twigs of box, holly, myrtle, rosemary, and other evergreens. For a copper or two, they sprinkled the hands and face of anyone they met. In every house, every room was sprinkled with New Year's water, and the inmates, who were often still in bed, were wished a happy New Year. The doors of closed houses were also sprinkled with water. The verse was sung during the sprinkling.

In certain parts of Wales, this custom is called *dwr newy* (literally, new water). The exact meaning of the phrase, "levy dew," is unknown although there have been attempts to trace it to *llef I Dduw* (Welsh for "cry of God"). This seems to be an imposition of a Christian interpretation on an older custom. Although the fair maid is now equated with the version, Owen thinks it likely that this custom derives from "an early well-cult made acceptable to medieval Christianity by its association with the Virgin and perpetuated both by the desire to wish one's neighbor well at the beginning of a new year and by the small monetary payment involved."

I first heard this song on an NPR "Winter Solstice" show, sung by the Festival of Light and Song, a female *a cappella* musical group. Their version omitted the first verse and began with the two verses about the fair maid followed by this chorus:

> For we have brought fresh water
> All from the well so clear
> To wish you and your company
> A joyful happy year.

Wassailing Songs

Like the New Year carolers of the Ukraine, wassailers in the British Isles go from house to house, singing songs that ask for a blessing of abundance upon the household. This is a magical service, for which they are compensated with generous food and drink.

Often they carry around a decorated punch bowl, dressed up with garlands and ribbons. Wassail is an old Saxon toast, perhaps as old as the fifth century, meaning "Be thou hale" or "in good health." It derives from the same root word found in health and holistic.

Wassailing also refers to the custom of going out to the trees in the orchard to honor them for providing the fruit used to make the cider. One tree is selected to represent them all. Its branches are dipped in the cider, a piece of cake soaked in cider is placed in its branches, and some of the cider is sprinkled around its roots. Sometimes mummers perform ritual dances, showing the tree how to produce more fruit; in Somerset, people joined hands and danced around the tree in a ring, singing a song. Here is one such song:

Here's to thee, old apple tree
when thou may bud
and thou may blow
and thou may have apples enow.

There are many versions of this wassailing song. I've provided the more common lyrics and the music here. I like this variation because of the affectionate references to the farm animals and the crops. It seems clear that these songs were improvised on the spot and adapted to suit the names of the subjects.

Wassail, wassail, all over the town!
Our toast it is white and our ale it is brown
Our bowl it is made of the white maple tree
With the wassailing bowl we'll drink to thee.

So here is to Broad May and to her broad horn
May God send our Master a good crop of corn
And a good crop of corn that we may all see
With the wassailing bowl we'll drink to thee.

And here is to Fillpail and to her left ear
Pray God send our mistress a happy New Year
And a happy New Year as e'er she did see
With our wassailing bowl we'll drink to thee.

This is the version sung on *The Christmas Revels* recording as a traditional wassail song from Gloucestershire. This recording also includes the other familiar wassailing song ("Here we come a-wassailing among the leaves so green...") and an Apple Tree Wassail from Somerset.

Mother Berta's Coming to Town

The Greenwood Singers, a Seattle pagan chorus, wrote new words to be sung to the tune of "Santa Claus is Coming to Town," for which J. Fred Coots wrote the music and Steven W. Posch-Coward wrote the original lyrics.

You better watch out when winter comes night
You better not doubt, I'm telling you why.
Mother Berta's coming to town!

She carries a sack made out of a skin
She dumps the toys out and stuffs the kids in,
Mother Berta's coming to town!

She rides on Ashurskeggi
A goat whose back is strong.
Her beard is long and scraggly
And her tail is ten feet long!

With six or eight horns, a moustache or two,
Make no mistake, she's coming for you!
Mother Berta's coming to town!

She knows with whom you're sleeping,
She knows with whom you wake,
She knows each thought you're thinking
So don't think, for Goddess sake!

So when the winds howl way up in the sky
Listen as she and Skeggi pass by.
Mother Berta's coming,
Mother Berta's coming,
Yes, Mother Berta's coming to town!

References

Attwater, Donald, *The Penguin Dictionary of Saints*, Penguin, second edition, 1983

Bernheimer, Richard, *Wild Men of the Middle Ages*, Octagon, 1970

Blackburn, Bonnie and Leofranc Holford-Strevens, *The Oxford Companion to the Year*, Oxford University Press, 1999

Bright, Marilyn, *The Christmas Cookbook*, Appletree Press, Harper Collins, 1993

Budapest, Z, *The Grandmother of Time*, Harper and Row, 1989

Carroll, Lewis, updated with an introduction and notes by Martin Gardner, *The Annotated Alice*, Wings Books, 1960

Cumont, Franz, *The Mysteries of Mithra*, Dover, 1956

Davidson, Alan, *Oxford Companion to Food*, Oxford University Press, 1999

Ellis, Normandi, "New Year Magic," *SageWoman*, Samhain, 1999

Ellis, Normandi, *Feasts of Light: Celebrations for the Seasons of Life based on the Egyptian Goddess Mysteries*, Quest, 1999

Farias, Helen, "Holler and Holle," *The Advent Sunwheel,* Juno's Peacock Press, 1989; reprint, Priestess of Swords Press, 2002 [order from www.schooloftheseasons.com]

Farias, Helen, "The Magical Ladies of the Thirteen Nights," *The Beltane Papers*, Issue 2, Samhain, 1992

Farias, Helen, "Women of the Sky," *Octava*, Yule, 1986.

Farias, Helen, *The Advent Sunwheel*, Juno's Peacock Press 1989; reprinted, Priestess of Swords Press, 2003 [order from www.schooloftheseasons.com]

Field, Carol, *Celebrating Italy*, William Morrow and Company, 1990

Fitzgerald, Waverly, "Playing Snapdragon," *The Beltane Papers*, Issue 2, Samhain, 1992

Gimbutas, Marija, *Goddesses and Gods of Old Europe*, Thames and Hudson, 1982

Gimbutas, Marija, *The Language of the Goddess*, San Francisco: Harper and Row, 1989

Ginzburg, Carlo, translated by Raymond Rosenthal, *Ecstasies: Deciphering the Witches' Sabbath*, Pantheon, 1991

Granquist, Susan, "Lucy Fest," www.irminsul.org/arc/001sg.html

Graves, Robert, *The Greek Myths*, Penguin, 1955

Greenwood Singers, *Yule* [out of print]

Hardie, Dee, *Hollyhocks, Lambs and Other Passions: A Memoir of Thornhill Farm*, New York: Atheneum, 1985

Hoever, Reverend Hugo, editor, *Lives of the Saints*, Catholic Book Publishing Company, 1965

Hole, Christina, *A Dictionary of British Folk Customs*, Paladin Books, 1978

Hottes, Alfred Carl, *1001 Christmas Facts and Fancies*, NY: De La Mare, 1937

Humphrey's research was described in an article, "Christmas Star was a comet seen in 5 BCE, says scientist" by David L Chandler, *Daily News*, December 21, 1991

Karas, Sheryl Ann, *The Solstice Evergreen*, Aslan, 1991

Kelly, Mary B, *Goddesses and Their Offspring*, NY: Binghamton, 1990

Kelly, Mary B, *Goddess Embroideries of Eastern Europe*, Studiobooks, Box 23, McLean NY 13102

Kightly, Charles, *The Perpetual Almanack of Folklore*, Thames & Hudson, 1987

Lang, Jenifer Harvey, editor, *Larousse Gastronomique*, Crown, 1984

Matthews, John, *The Winter Solstice*, Quest, 1998

Miles, Clement A., *Christmas in Ritual and Tradition*, London: Unwin, 1912; republished by Gale Research, Detroit, 1968

Monagahan, Patricia, *The Book of Goddesses and Heroines*, Llewellyn, 1990

Monaghan, Patricia, *O Mother Sun! A New View of the Cosmic Feminine*, Crossing Press, 1994

Murphy, Charlie, Jamie Sieber, and the Total Experience Gospel Choir, "Canticles of Light," Out Front Music, 1984

Nathan, Joan, *The Jewish Holiday Kitchen*, NY: Schoken Books, 1988

Nelson, Gertrud Mueller, *To Dance with God: Family Ritual and Community Celebration*, Paulist Press, 1986

Owen, Trefor, *Welsh Folk Customs*, Llandysul, Dyged: Gomer Press, 1987

Parke, H W, *Festivals of the Athenians*, Cornell University Press, 1977

Scharfenberg, Horst, *Cuisines of Germany*, Poseidon Press, 1989

Sheraton, Mimi, *Visions of Sugar Plums*, Harper Collins, 1986

Simetti, Mary Taylor, *On Persephone's Island*, Knopf, 1986

Spicer, Dorothy Gladys, *From an English Oven*, 1948; reissued by several publishers

Spicer, Dorothy Gladys, *The Book of Festivals*, 1937; reissued by several publishers

Van Hevlingen, Andy, *The Herb Companion*, Dec/Jan, 1992/1993

Walker, Barbara, *Encyclopedia of Myths and Secrets*, Harper and Row, 1983

Walters, Brent, director of the Centre for Early Christian Studies, San Jose State University, http://www.didache.com

Warner, Marina, *Alone of All Her Sex: The Myth and Cult of the Virgin Mary*, Vintage, 1976

Waskow, Arthur, *Seasons of Our Joy: A Modern Guide to the Jewish Holidays*, Beacon, 1982

Web Sites:

Revels tapes: www.revels.org

www.udayton.edu/mary/questions/yq/yq28.html
(information on Our Lady of Solitude)

www.stnicholascenter.org

www.candlegrove.com/sollink/

Music:

Richardson, Allen L., *Sing We Now of Christmas*, Cincinnati, OH: The Willis Music Co (except for the Lucia lyrics)

Illustrations:

Cover: *The Christmas Tree*, Emily Mary Osborn (British, 1828–1925), 1864

About This Book

This is one of a series of books inspired by my love for and collection of folklore and customs associated with seasonal holidays, an obsession which began when I was a lonely sophomore at Reed College in Oregon and spent hours in the library poring through the *Funk and Wagnall's Dictionary of Folklore and Mythology* and Chambers' *Book of Days*. I was especially curious about how certain symbols appeared in the traditions of different cultures and religions (my declared major was Symbolism) and wanted to understand what those had to do with the holidays.

It turns out the answer is simple: holidays usually reflect what's going on in the natural world at that particular moment in the round of the year. Religions superimposed their own belief systems upon those existing symbols, for instance, placing the birth of the Son of God at the same time as the celebration of the rebirth of the Sun at Winter Solstice. Of course, these holidays are keyed in to the natural cycles of the Western world, rather than those of countries lying south of the equator, but often cultures as far away from Europe as China and India have similar customs and celebrations.

Because of my research and my association with calendar scholar Helen Farias, I have a great collection of books about holidays and am always adding to my knowledge. Most of the research for this book was done with those sources.

The first version of this book was written before the Internet. Now it's quite possible to see what Wikipedia knows about formerly obscure holidays and also how people in those cultures and countries are celebrating this year. Since such a wealth of information exists and is constantly being updated (and disappearing) on the internet, I've tried to focus here on making the common themes clear.

More information can be found on my website, Living in Season, where I also have a calendar for each month listing detailed information about holidays, plus longer articles on the seasonal holidays: www.livinginseason.com/

My interest in seasonal holidays spilled out into an interest into natural time, leading to my book, *Slow Time: Reclaiming the Rhythm of the Seasons*: www.livinginseason.com/slow-time/

From Waverly Fitzgerald

Fiction
St. John's Wood
Chelsea
Mayfair
Grover Square
Queen of Shadows
Hard Rain

As Waverly Curtis
co-authored with Curt Colbert
Dial C for Chihuahua
Chihuahua Confidential
The Big Chihuahua
The Chihuahua Always Sniffs Twice
A Chihuahua in Every Stocking
The Case of the Naughty Santa

Nonfiction
Slow Time: Recovering the Natural Rhythm of Life
Celebrating Spring Equinox
Celebrating Summer Solstice
Celebrating Autumn Equinox
Celebrating Winter Solstice

www.waverlyfitzgerald.com

Printed in Great Britain
by Amazon